The Avalanche Expertise Project

Canadian Expert Avalanche Decision Making

Developed as a tool through to 2024 for the advancement of decision making aimed at those involved in avalanche terrain.

Tony Walker helicourse@gmail.com

"It is impossible to learn that which one thinks one already knows." – Epictetus

Table of Contents

AEP Preface -5

Introduction - The Avalanche Expertise Project -7

List of Scenarios -9

Rescue in the Rockies - Rescue risks, judgment, and survival -10

Angels Speak - Pressure, judgment, risk, and consequences -20

The Plot Thickens – Heli-skiing uncertainty amidst unpredictable terrain.- 31

Go Fetch - Balancing Avalanche Risk and Productivity - 52

Pockets and Pipes - Balancing Risk, Responsibility, and Thrilll- 65

Yes Boss - Confidence, Consequences, and Leadership Dynamics - 78

Bada Boom - Strategic Avalanche Control Amid Pressure - 90

What's for Launch? – Avalauncher Decisions: Navigating Instability Risks.- 98

Stepping Off - Avalanche Control: Assessing Hidden Triggers.- 106

Count to Five - choosing terrain for a group - 116

The Gray Zone -Alphas that need direction - 132

Bummer Dude – summer limited options and hazards - 148

Cake Walk – changing conditions and plans -164

The White Canvas – buried layers and triggers - 176

Mother's Surprise – Risk, Instincts, and survival in snow - 194

The Balance – Balancing Risk and Adrenaline in Unpredictable Conditions - 206

Dragon Buttons - Navigating Uncertainty: Instinct, Terrain, Risk - 224

Sled Bowling – using terrain appropriately - 238

Did you See That? - Unexplainable evidence of instability - 246

Tip Toes – unprecedented conditions and influence - 254

AEP Participation Request - 266

OpenAI Participation - 268

An Incomplete Cross Reference of scenarios - 269

Glossary - 270

Thoughts and Quotes – Snippets of Wisdom from Experts - 271

"Experience is the hardest kind of teacher. It gives you the test first and the lesson afterward."

AEP Preface
Paradigms of the Masters

This Project is a collection of wisdom from the experts. What they have accomplished is not easy and neither will be your acquisition of expertise.

Avalanche experts of 20 to 40 years' experience were asked about a time when their expertise was challenged.

From those interviews, a scenario was developed that was reviewed and approved by the expert.

The expert would then suggest another expert to interview.

You can use these scenarios to build your intuitive wisdom. Follow the directions, take the time, do the work, and you will be rewarded with higher level thinking.

"Avoid stupidity before seeking brilliance" Charlie Munger

"Believe it possible. You may be mistaken." Oliver Cromwell.

Introduction - The Avalanche Expertise Project

The 2005 paper by Laura Adams (A Systems Approach to Human Factors and Expert Decision-Making Within Canadian Avalanche Phenomena) recommended "critical thinking training to enhance the development of critical thinking, situational awareness, and metacognition for those in the avalanche industry". In response to that suggestion, the Avalanche Expertise Project (AEP) was started in 2023.

Cognitive Task Analysis (CTA) is used to gather the wisdom of experts and deliver it to others. One of the challenges of expertise is the curse of knowledge, the inability to understand just how complicated and nuanced one's thinking has become. This inability can interfere with the transfer of wisdom (up to 70%). CTA uses various strategies to capture both the explicit knowledge, implicit knowledge and the thinking that experts use to carry out complex tasks.

The CTA method involves the identification of an expert, who is then interviewed about an occasion where their expertise made a difference in the outcome. This recollection is then probed to capture context, cues, goals, expectations, and options. The recollection (or story) is then transcribed and both the interviewer and the expert review it to ensure it is accurate and complete.

For educational purposes, the AEP creates an anonymized story from a transcribed interview with the Expert using their own words. This story is presented as a simulation, stopping at defined points to ask the learner a "What would you do now" question. They are then asked to reflect on the expert's actions. This technique enhances the development of critical thinking and the recognition of cues, assessments, potential errors, and options. Different than case studies which delineate a problem, the AEP drives the participant to recognize the situation that needs addressing. Following the reflection, the learner then reads the of the Expert's actions and thoughts.

The Expert's Reflection section at the end of each scenario helps the learner to develop a deeper understanding of the thoughts and motivations of the expert in that scenario and in the avalanche world as a whole.

The avalanche doesn't know you're an expert.

List of Scenarios

Organized in order of when the interview took place

1 Rescue in the Rockies –	entering unknown terrain
2 Angels Speak –	nonevent feedback and bias
3 The Plot Thickens –	planning in heliskiing
4 Go Fetch –	assessment at distance
5 Pockets and Pipes –	choosing terrain for a group
6 Yes Boss –	ski cutting & bad ideas
7 Bada Boom –	explosives control
8 What's for Launch? –	assessing stability remotely
9 Stepping Off –	ski cutting with a plan
10 Count to Five –	choosing terrain for a group
11 The Gray Zone –	alphas that need direction
12 Bummer Dude –	summer options and hazards
13 Cake Walk –	changing conditions and plans
14 The White Canvas –	buried layers and triggers
15 Mother's Surprise –	terrain choice
16 The Balance –	pressure to ski with DPWL
17 Dragon Buttons –	DPWL and subordinates
18 Sled Bowling -	using terrain appropriately
19 Did You See That?	unexplainable evidence
20 Tip Toes -	unprecedented conditions

Rescue in the Rockies - Rescue risks, judgment, and survival

Read the following scenario developed from an interview with an expert and stop at the decision point question as indicated by the statement...

"Write down your cues, goals, and what are you thinking/doing."

The following is very important and is how you will learn using this method.

Put yourself in the place of the expert and write down what you would be thinking and or doing if you were in that situation. **If you don't take the time to do this... you won't learn.**

Note that the information in the scenario might be incomplete, much the same as it would be in the real world.

<u>Do not skip ahead</u>. Reading ahead to see what the expert has done before you have put your thoughts down, will negate the value of this exercise.

After you have put your thoughts on paper refer to the next page "Thoughts of the Expert...". Have you differed or missed something? Think about that.

Continue reading the scenario sections, writing down your thoughts, and reading those of the expert until you come to the end. Reflect about the situation. In the same position, would you make the same decisions? What would be the outcome of those decisions?

Read the Expert's reflections to gain context and deeper understanding.

During your review of the expert's scenario and their thoughts, write down 5 key points. Compare your 5 to those developed by ChatGPT-4.

If you have any questions or comments, please reach out to
helicourse@gmail.com

Rescue in the Rockies 1

It is midwinter in the Rockies. You lead four other members of the rescue organization and have just been called to fly in by helicopter to an avalanche accident. A group of 6 back country skiers in their early 20's had been ski touring into a large alpine cirque with huge snow covered slopes on three sides. It is big terrain. They were caught by a size three hard slab avalanche that started from the upper center portion of the cirque and ran for 400 metres. Not all were involved, some were partially buried, and one was missing. The partial burials were either self-rescued or dug out by those not involved. A rescue beacon search for the missing skier turned up nothing.

A member of the group raced back to the trailhead and drove to the nearest phone and alerted the rescue organization who fly into the accident site by helicopter. The first team of rescuers to arrive conduct a beacon search has reveals nothing, and a probe line is started. Dusk is falling. Your group will be the third and last group of rescuers delivered on site that day. The helicopter flies you into the valley where you have been only in the summer. You can see the entire cirque, the avalanche, and the probe line that you will be integrated into.

(1). Write down your cues, goals, and what are you thinking/doing.

<u>Do not skip ahead.</u>

Thoughts and Actions of the Expert 1

The winter snowpack, its layers, and reason for triggering avalanches. Use previous analogues – what have I seen this winter that is similar to here?

The shape of the valley which is a large basin. This means that there is possibility for more avalanches to come off the top and into the valley.

The threat those avalanches might pose to the rescuers as they continue to probe.

The huge slope above the lower half of the deposit, where the probe line will eventually get to.

The probable runout of that huge slope if it avalanches and definite marks, such as an exposed rock, on the ground to reference its likely boundaries.

The boulder is a hard stop. Do not pass that and put yourself in danger from above.

Rescue in the Rockies 2

You are now part of the probe line. The helicopter has left but everyone has ski gear and headlamps so skiing out in the dark is the exit plan. Flying in you observed a large avalanche slope hanging above the lower half of the deposit. You also observe a large boulder protruding above the surface of the snow, right where the hangfire above starts to threaten the deposit you are probing. You probe and probe. The deposit is quite deep, up to 3 metres, and it takes a long time – time in fact is running out for the victim. It gets dark and the probing continues. Eventually, 5-6 hours after the avalanche, you find yourself and the rest of the rescuers at the boulder you had observed flying in.

(2). Write down your cues, goals, and what are you thinking/doing.

Do not skip ahead.

Thoughts and Actions of the Expert 2

This is the landmark that is a hard stop. It is dangerous to go past it.

Tell the group that your assessment on the way in has made this a stopping point especially because it is dark and danger from above would be unseen and there would be no time to react.

You are not going below this until the hangfire is dealt with (in this case it was helibombed the next day and a further 2 metres of snow was piled on top of the existing deposit coming very close to the mark. The victim was discovered by probe in the old debris where they hadn't probed, 3 metres down).

End of Scenario

Reflect on this ...

(3) What would you do if the group decided to keep going past the mark?

(4) What is your primary motivation in rescue situations like this?

(5) What is your paradigm (describe your thinking) when showing up at a rescue?

(6) What would you have done if you were the junior member of the team?

(7) What about uncertainties?

Expert's response to questions 3 – 7

(3) What would you do if the group decided to keep going past the mark? Tell the group that you will wait for them in a safe location.

(4) The primary motivation is not making the find, go home, and get it over with. The primary motivation is safety of the rescuers. The hangfire could have been discounted because of the sense of urgency of a buried person. "Charge ahead with lives at risk!" But that's a rookie mistake. It is how you get your rescue people hurt and if you lose the trust of your team then you're ineffective, so you have to model that behavior that you want to see followed.

To come home, to come home, which is the goal of every emergency response. You want to get the job done but first you want to come home. Job number one is to bring everybody home, job number two is to find the body.

(5) What is your paradigm (describe your thinking) when showing up at a rescue? Always do a global assessment – make sure you have the whole picture with as much detail as possible. Run scenarios in your mind. If this, then what...

(6) As a junior, I probably would have kept my mouth shut. Well, I mean I am not expert in this, I have to trust the people that are older, more experienced, more time in the mountains, but by that time I'd come to have some self-confidence. If you feel strongly don't be afraid to speak up. You can use body language to do that. For example, just not going into the area which you think is dangerous.

(7) Of course, one has uncertainties. In this case "Am I being too conservative?" Ask yourself "How solid is this choice given all the information that is available to me?"

Q: How about if you got pulled into a valley that you hadn't been into. You got a call and there's some wreck over there and you had no experience in the valley. You come in by helicopter, sneaking underneath the clouds that hide the terrain above, and there's the debris. What would your decision making have been then?

A: Tough, really tough.

Q: Can you play that scenario through?

A: You know there's potential there, but you can't really see what it is you can't evaluate it

Q: So, what do you do?

A: Make sure everyone goes home that night.

Q: How do you do that?

A: Maybe you don't go up there that day, maybe you wait, wait until the weather gets better.

End of the Expert's Reflections

What are the five key points you developed?

Key Points Generated by ChatGPT-4

Note: OpenAI has attached the following to its webpage "ChatGPT can make mistakes. Check important info." Do you agree with what has been summarized?

Assess and Prioritize Rescuer Safety:

Ensure the safety of rescuers takes precedence over the urgency of finding the victim. When assessing the scene, identify potential secondary avalanche risks, such as hangfire above the debris field. Use clear landmarks, such as the protruding boulder in this scenario, to establish non-negotiable safety boundaries.

Thorough Situational Analysis:

Conduct a comprehensive assessment of the avalanche site, considering both current conditions and past analogues to understand the snowpack and potential triggers.

Run through various scenarios in your mind to prepare for different outcomes and reactions.

Effective Communication and Decision Making:

Communicate clearly and assertively with the rescue team, especially when stopping the probe line at identified danger points. Explain the rationale behind safety decisions to ensure team understanding and compliance.

If the group decides to proceed past a designated safety mark, communicate your decision to stay in a safe location and wait, modeling the behavior you expect.

Adaptability and Openness to Uncertainty:

Acknowledge and manage uncertainties. Constantly question whether decisions are too conservative or too risky based on the information available.

In unfamiliar terrain or when visibility is poor, consider postponing the mission until conditions improve to ensure the safety of all rescuers.

Leadership and Learning:

As a junior member, trust the judgment of more experienced team members but don't hesitate to voice concerns if you feel strongly about a safety issue.

Use body language to communicate hesitancy if you feel uncomfortable with the decisions being made, reinforcing your commitment to safety.

The key is to realize it that it can happen to you.

Angels Speak - Pressure, judgment, risk, and consequences

Read the following scenario developed from an interview with an expert and stop at the decision point question as indicated by the statement...

"Write down your cues, goals, and what are you thinking/doing."

The following is very important and is how you will learn using this method.

Put yourself in the place of the expert and write down what you would be thinking and or doing if you were in that situation. **If you don't take the time to do this... you won't learn.**

Note that the information in the scenario might be incomplete, much the same as it would be in the real world.

<u>Do not skip ahead</u>. Reading ahead to see what the expert has done before you have put your thoughts down, will negate the value of this exercise.

After you have put your thoughts on paper refer to the next page "Thoughts of the Expert...". Have you differed or missed something? Think about that.

Continue reading the scenario sections, writing down your thoughts, and reading those of the expert until you come to the end. Reflect about the situation. In the same position, would you make the same decisions? What would be the outcome of those decisions?

Read the Expert's reflections to gain context and deeper understanding.

During your review of the expert's scenario and their thoughts, write down 5 key points. Compare your 5 to those developed by ChatGPT-4.

If you have any questions or comments, please reach out to
helicourse@gmail.com

Angels Speak 1

It is mid-winter at the coastal heliski company, and you have just returned to work after being off for a week with a bad cold. You know that you have to be very sensitive to the economics of the operation as you are the guide in charge of this single group in the 212 helicopter. The flight time is measured in hours and is divided into tenths, each tenth being hundreds of dollars. Efficiency in the industry and at the operation is measured by the number of flying hours divided by the vertical skied by the clients.

You take off for your first run and it is a long flight, 15 minutes or so, to get to the terrain you want to ski. The flying is iffy, one of those typical coastal days with a little too much moisture in the air. The day is fairly warm, and the alpine is obscured by cloud.

You fly up to the area where you can do tree runs in the transition zone you use when you're not able to access above treeline (which you can't do that day). The clock is ticking as you look for your preferred run, but you can't land where you want because of the lack of flight visibility. So, you fly around the corner to another run that you are familiar with. It starts in the transition zone and goes below tree line, a fairly lengthy run of about 1000 meters. As you fly in, there is cloud around, the regular landing is obscured. You are looking for a place where we can see an alternative landing stake. You look everywhere for it, a hump where you can land below the clouds. You aren't in the cloud, but you know how clouds move around. It is challenging. You have a very experienced 212 pilot with you who suddenly says, "Hey, I see a landing stake. I can put you there."

(1). Write down your cues, goals, and what are you thinking/doing.

<u>Do not skip ahead.</u>

Thoughts and Actions of the Expert 1

I am happy to have stopped flying around burning money.

"What am I going to ski?"

What is the terrain and the consequence of an avalanche?"

I want a look at the run.

The winter snowpack, its layers, and reason for triggering avalanches. Use previous analogues – "What have I seen this winter that is similar to here?"

Angels Speak 2

By then you have already spent a lot of flying time, so without having enough of a chance to really look at the area you say to the pilot, "OK, put her down there." Another guide has put this stake in, and you know you are in the proximity of your selected run. You land and exit. The helicopter leaves and goes to park on the pickup, very far down in the bottom of the valley, a thousand vertical metres below.

Because you have been paying attention to the snowpack all winter, you know there are a few layers in it. The coastal snowpack is much more stable than the interior and you know it's rare that you actually really have to worry about stuff. So, you find yourself at this place which is not the normal top landing of the run but put in by some other guide. In order to get to the regular run, you have to go down a little and then cross the 200 m by 200 m convex slope with a cliff below it. The skiing will be great as there is 30 or 40 centimeters of fresh snow.

(2). Write down your cues, goals, and what are you thinking/doing.

<u>Do not skip ahead.</u>

Thoughts and Actions of the Expert 2

There is potential here for the slope to slide with large consequences because the slope is above a cliff and is unsupported.

I am suspicious of the snowpack and need more information.

It is best for me to check it out and keep the clients safe, waiting on the landing.

I leave instructions for the group to come one at a time after I cross and give them the signal of a raised ski pole.

Angels Speak 3

So, you tell the group to stop on the landing and wait for your signal to follow. You go down about 150 meters in length, and 100 meters in elevation loss. You don't dig a huge profile, but because of the new snow you do a quick 5 second hand shear test, and it comes out easy.

(3). Write down your cues, goals, and what are you thinking/doing.

<u>Do not skip ahead.</u>

Thoughts and Actions of the Expert 3

The easy hand shear, convex slope, nonstandard route, and big consequence heightens your Spidey sense. The clients are put into danger. Maybe don't ski this.

Maybe I should ski it because I am far below the group who are on the landing, it is deep snow, the helicopter is far down in the valley, and I have been sick and am weaker than I normally am.

Because of the easy hand shear indicating avalanche danger, maybe climb up to the group and call the machine back, fly to another run with the attendant delay, expense, and damage to ego that that decision entails.

I turn around and grudgingly hike up in 40 centimeters of new snow. I am sweating like a pig by the time I get to the top.

Back on the landing I choose not to hike with the group a longer but safer route to the run I wanted to ski (after all it is called heli skiing not heli walking).

I call the pilot in. Sound like a loser. The helicopter comes all the way back up from the bottom of the valley, plucks me off, lands me somewhere else and the day proceeds.

End of Scenario

The Expert's Reflections ...

I landed at the end of the day, and I told the boss what had happened. He hugged me and said, "Thank you very much you did the right thing, don't worry about the flying time."

Two days later, there was an avalanche on that same layer, about 500 meters away and a valley over. A size 3, in which the guide got taken down all the way, had a punctured lung, and broken bones but survived it.

I could not cross over to my desired run by skiing the top of the convex slope which is the safe thing to do. The way the slope was and the way the helicopter was perched I had to go down and through the middle of it to get to the main run.

So, add a little sun effect or little wind effect, the tension in the snowpack is more of a slab. The convex slope wasn't slabby, it was loose snow. That was the lure to not turn around to go back after I started skiing down, because it wasn't this happy happy slab. I would probably not even have gone as far as 150 m if it was a slab.

On the top I said to the group, "If I'm on the other side." I actually didn't say if, I said "When I'm on the other side" because at that time I still thought I was gonna get to the other side.

Working in risk management, you always imagine the worst. Like this is part of my life that you visualize the worst outcome without getting anxious. I mean you're a professional right, so you visualize the worst outcome, and you compare against it. Like you know what could happen and in order to avoid that happening, you follow these subsequent steps when you are guiding.

So, I think when I stood there, I visualized the outcome if it goes sideways and I saw me, or a client, tumbling down that convex cliff.

I think I was uncomfortable the whole way through as soon as the pilot said he had a stake, and he could put me there. I felt "Oh shit, I haven't really had a good look at that slope" and yet I overrode this and said "Yeah, put me there." because I need to get the bloody machine down on the ground as soon as possible.

I had the data. I should have listened to my first weird feeling when I was sitting in the front seat and when the pilot said, "I can land you there", I should have reacted then and said "No way. I haven't had a good look yet."

I had already tossed all kinds of run options out that were not possible.

You always need angels, right? So, technically the worst that could have happened was that I overrode my first feeling and landed and as I was 100 meters down, it would have released on me, and I would be toast. I guess that day I had a little angel that I listened to. I was still trying to push just a little bit.

You have the knowledge of the snowpack in your bones as it grows during the winter because you follow it all the time, even on your time off.

I think the human factors really come in - the pressure of having to perform. Earlier in my career I would have been much more hesitant to just call a helicopter back up and pluck me off because I would have been embarrassed to incur the extra cost. Afraid to not be accepted.

I think in general with every incident, with every accident, you hear about, it just gives you a more visceral feeling of what the consequences could be. I openly admit I am now a total chicken shit. Like I pull back real soon. I really don't care about the pressure of the clients. In fact, if they bitch about skiing not steep enough, I ski flatter, but I don't stop for such a long stretch that their legs burn, and they stop bitching because they are out of breath. I have no performance ego anymore.

Know yourself and your ego almost above your technical knowledge, because I think that has probably killed more people. To take that risk. Lots of traps out there.

If the novice is not self-confident enough to speak up, that's another one of the heuristic traps. Even the least experienced, if you have butterflies in your stomach, please speak up because maybe those five testosterone filled guys leading the day are going to miss something that the inexperienced person feels subconsciously.

You know, you have to be an influence that is calming.

The goal on top of the slope is to safely deliver a great product for the client.

End of the Expert's Reflections

What are the five key points you developed?

Key Points Generated by ChatGPT-4

Note: OpenAI has attached the following to its webpage "ChatGPT can make mistakes. Check important info." Do you agree with what has been summarized?

Safety First and Trust Your Instincts:

Prioritize safety over all other concerns, including economic pressures. Listen to your gut feelings and initial reactions. If something feels off, address it immediately don't proceed under pressure.

Thorough Assessment of the Terrain and Snowpack:

Conduct a detailed evaluation of the snowpack and terrain before committing to a run. Be aware of the snowpack layers, recent weather conditions, and potential avalanche triggers. If visibility or knowledge of the terrain is insufficient, err on the side of caution. Choose safer routes even if they are less exciting or involve more effort.

Efficient Communication and Client Management:

Clearly communicate with your team and clients about the plan and any changes due to safety concerns. Use clear signals and instructions to manage client movement safely. In this scenario, instruct clients to wait for your signal before proceeding.

Decision-Making Under Pressure:

Make decisions based on safety rather than economic considerations, even if it involves additional costs or logistical challenges. In this case, calling the helicopter back to relocate was the safer option despite the expense.

Learn from Experience and Stay Humble:

Reflect on past experiences and learn from them. Acknowledge that it's okay to change plans and prioritize safety over ego or the perceived need to perform. As experience grows, so should the ability to make conservative decisions confidently.

All the information you're bringing in determines how you'll approach every situation.

The Plot Thickens – Heli-skiing uncertainty amidst unpredictable terrain.

Read the following scenario developed from an interview with an expert and stop at the decision point question as indicated by the statement...

"Write down your cues, goals, and what are you thinking/doing.."

The following is very important and is how you will learn using this method.

Put yourself in the place of the expert and write down what you would be thinking and or doing if you were in that situation. **If you don't take the time to do this... you won't learn.**

Note that the information in the scenario might be incomplete, much the same as it would be in the real world.

<u>Do not skip ahead</u>. Reading ahead to see what the expert has done before you have put your thoughts down, will negate the value of this exercise.

After you have put your thoughts on paper refer to the next page "Thoughts of the Expert...". Have you differed or missed something? Think about that.

Continue reading the scenario sections, writing down your thoughts, and reading those of the expert until you come to the end. Reflect about the situation. In the same position, would you make the same decisions? What would be the outcome of those decisions?

Read the Expert's reflections to gain context and deeper understanding.

During your review of the expert's scenario and their thoughts, write down 5 key points. Compare your 5 to those developed by ChatGPT-4.

If you have any questions or comments, please reach out to
helicourse@gmail.com

The Plot Thickens 1

You are a heliski guide and have been working several years for the operation which has a huge tenure (perhaps the BC Coastal mountains or the far north of the province, or the Himalaya). Your assignment is to take a private group accompanied by a junior guide into a large remote area. Neither of you are intimately familiar with the zone, much of it still unexplored so there are no run maps or photos. You have to plan your day. The weather is not great, with scudding clouds and snow showers forecast. You have a large map of the tenure on the wall and have to figure out which runs you will be able to fly to and ski safely. The weather report is indicating a southwesterly flow.

(1). Write down your cues, goals, and what are you thinking/doing.

Do not skip ahead

Thoughts and Actions of the Expert 1

You have to guess but you can think of it on the macro scale. You could get close to the map and look at the runs individually but in these situations, try standing about eight feet back from the map (distance depending on the scale of the map) and look at the terrain as a whole. Consider the flow of the weather that day. Where's the weather coming from? Is it southwesterly flow? Now imagine a southwesterly flow across that terrain on that macro scale that you're looking at when you stand back and you can start to guess the places that holes might open up in that weather in the lee of large features.

You have the trick of looking at the isobar lines and knowing that the winds run generally parallel to those and the tightness of the lines will represent strength of the wind. You can deduce flow from a 500 Mb picture or looking at weather models if that is all you have got. Generally, they will line up with what the winds are going to do over time and you can deduce what is happening with flow.

Sometimes flight times to get to some of these spots may be long, so there's a risk that you'll fly to the location and find visibility insufficient to fly and ski there, you have to make that decision and accept that risk or not.

Step outside after looking at the map, the 500 millibar picture and the weather models and simply feel the wind to see what direction is blowing at the elevation you're at. then look up into the sky and watch which way the clouds are moving to get a sense of what wind direction is at higher altitude to see if that corroborates or disagrees with the picture you've developed so far.

The Plot Thickens 2

You have selected your area to ski and get in the helicopter and start flying in the chosen direction.

(2). Write down your cues, goals, and what are you thinking/doing.

> Do not skip ahead

Thoughts and Actions of the Expert 2

Have your senses turned on and continually pick up information.

Several times ask the pilot the wind direction and speed because he can compare his ground and air speed and tell you that.

Continue to do this as you climb through elevations to see if wind speed and/or direction varies.

Use visual clues of the wind on the snow in the terrain to see what the wind has been doing in terms of its direction and its intensity.

Looking where the wind moves snow. Loading is a big factor in certain types of avalanche problems particularly storm and wind slabs.

Either confirm or refute your thesis about what the winds did previously and are doing presently.

The Plot Thickens 3

You know there is persistent weak layer (PWL) in the snowpack. The terrain you are working in is large and relatively unskied so there is little information about the layer on any specific run. It is a long and therefore expensive flight out to your chosen area. The recent storm was quite windy but finished with no wind, the gently falling blanket of snow covered most of the evidence for your thesis about the wind effect.

(3). Write down your cues, goals, and what are you thinking/doing.

<u>Do not skip ahead</u>

Thoughts and Actions of the Expert 3

When my uncertainty rises, your willingness to ski a range of terrain should shrink down to more conservative terrain until you can collect more data. If you can't get enough of that data to confirm theories about PWL and to go into different terrain then simply default to much more conservative terrain where it doesn't matter whether you get it right or wrong.

So, in other words you always have the option to choose terrain that is so conservative and so safe that it almost doesn't matter what the conditions are. You can edge further and further toward that kind of terrain if uncertainties are too great to be more specific about the terrain.

The Plot Thickens 4

You have made the flight out to the area in marginal weather. The flight visibility occasionally gets close to unflyable (less than 2 miles) and you are having a difficult time finding a run that is suitable for both flying and ski safety/quality.

(4). Write down your cues, goals, and what are you thinking/doing.

<u>Do not skip ahead</u>

Thoughts and Actions of the Expert 4

That must be a conversation with the pilot. The guide's side of that equation would be things like:

Can you see well enough to assess hazards on the run from the air?

Will you continue to see well enough to assess and avoid hazard when skiing down?

If visibility diminishes, will you still be able to manage the hazard?

On the pilot side of course is there enough visibility for me to get a safe landing?

Is there a safe place for the helicopter to park?

If the visibility changed with the machine shutdown, will it be able to fly away?

Is the pickup at low enough elevation that reference from trees is sufficient to pick the group up with a reasonable margin of visibility and safety?

The above could be a pretty long discussion between the guide and the pilot. If a long discussion is needed, just find a safe place to park and have the conversation without the distraction and cost of flying. Explore the options, but don't do it under pressure flying around spending money. Park, stop the clock, discuss.

When a decision needs time, give it time

Sometimes at some point, with only financial and not safety considerations, you take a punt, a risk, by flying into the field without the certainty of success. It might work, it might not. These financial risks need to be balanced against the need to deliver the product.

It would be rare especially in those questionable conditions to land without landing stakes. Visibility for the helicopter landing is paramount so in the absence of flags there must be sufficient natural reference or a landing would be inappropriate.

Remain aware that decisions can easily push into safety consequences. If you get there let's say, and you're feeling the financial pressure piece or client pressure and it's not as sunny as you'd hoped but it's workable, you might decide to start skiing. With changing conditions, that decision to start skiing could be the first hole in the Swiss cheese. (https://en.wikipedia.org/wiki/Swiss_cheese_model).

The Plot Thickens 5

You have made run selections with the pilot's involvement and are now skiing very safe terrain. The runs have excellent reference for the pilot to land even without landing stakes (which are put in after the first landing). It is quite flat and relatively boring skiing. The clients are becoming vociferous about the value for the money they have paid and want to ski the steeper and deeper slopes they can see around them.

(5). Write down your cues, goals, and what are you thinking/doing.

<u>Do not skip ahead</u>

Thoughts and Actions of the Expert 5

You empathize with the client and say "You know what I'm really sorry. I know you came to ski steep and deep, but this is what I'm comfortable skiing today. While your skiing enjoyment is very important to me, I have another priority that trumps that one and that is to get you home safely".

You continue to ski safer terrain until you become certain about the safety of the PWL.

The Plot Thickens 6

It has been a long time, the greater part of the season so far, that you have been skiing on that PWL and you continually hear negative comments about terrain selection from the clients. It has been a long period of not seeing any avalanche activity on the deep weak layer.

(6). Write down your cues, goals, and what are you thinking/doing.

<u>Do not skip ahead</u>

Thoughts and Actions of the Expert 6

Continue to ski that low angle terrain. It allows you to address that uncertainty and maintain a level of risk management.

Think about the duration and depth of the layer in the snowpack and its ability to heal over time but also the need for really good corroborating evidence to show that it is healing. This has to be more than just an absence of avalanche activity.

Look to be digging a lot of snow profiles to examine that layer in many different aspects and elevations to see how the snow crystal is progressing over time, at least in these limited samples. Even as you do this you know the terrain is so expansive that the pit only reveals information for that spot.

Watch the nearest neighbors to see what that PWL is doing in their areas because after what will happen with these layers is that they will wake up in you know in particular places. That's the harbinger of what is coming to other places soon after, so keep an eye on the neighbours as well.

Recognize that the digging of snow profiles to track the progress of that layer is statistically insignificant, you know the numbers of profiles that one can dig compared to the amount of terrain we're talking about (many square kilometres) is laughable. Just because the layer isn't found in a particular pit, doesn't mean it doesn't exist.

End of Scenario

The Expert's Reflections ...

A big part of what we do is daily recording of all our observations so it's all a matter of record. When I'm on weeks off, my morning reading always includes the INFOEX. That's how I keep my head inside of it. I don't let my head slip out of awareness of what's going on. A big part of the job is just this having your senses turned on all the time.

Knowing where the layers are is done by doing a meticulous job of tracking where it is when it first appears on the surface or perhaps more importantly, where you are certain it is not, then tracking where it survived before it got buried, and having good records of that.

We need to constantly question ourselves. We make predictions in our planning meetings and then must go into the field with our senses turned on and our minds open to our theories being right or wrong. Assuming we are correct in our predictions can get us into trouble.

More experienced older guides will ski flat terrain all day long more readily because they have seen enough to know the consequences if they get it wrong. I believe that guides reaction to any particular risk that they manage is directly related to the proximity that they have had to realizing the consequences of that risk.

Experienced guides grow accustomed to letting guests complain about the quality of the skiing. They have a more visceral understanding of the consequences if they get it wrong. They are less impacted emotionally by negative feedback from clients.

Experienced guides have enough experience to know "I can't outsmart this so I'm just a slave to it". Often younger guides that can do that for a little while, but they can't manage to keep entrenched in that really conservative mindset for the longer term, so they start to want to step up the terrain severity. This can be challenging to manage and may even require management to impose terrain restrictions on guides.

Sometimes we'll see people making decisions where priorities get mixed up and quality of the product comes before safety because of the perceived and real pressure that guides feel to deliver a really great experience that meets their clients' expectations. It's a really strong motivator. Giving guides better risk communication skills to deal with clients can help, but also ultimately this core understanding that if you can't get clients to understand that's OK, because they don't have the expertise that you do and you're just doing what's best for them.

I think variety of experience is really important. I also think that intensity of experience is also true for guiding. If you're in the same place, doing the same thing over and over again it's not going to be nearly as good as moving around, seeing different things, and doing being in unfamiliar situations a lot but always under the focused mentorship of really experienced people.

I do think that doing it by yourself is another important component. Ultimately, to learn, a person has to make their own decisions and live with the consequences. I also think that another piece that we haven't mentioned is the attitude of students and their openness to learning. Some people are open to being wrong and to learning and assimilating learning, and others not as much. That often has to do with that alchemy of the of the student teacher relationship.

I think a really key ingredient is the humility around thinking how much you know.

You can show uncertainty to colleagues and clients without killing their confidence in you. In fact, you can increase their confidence in you by being transparent about the things you know and the things you don't know and explaining how you manage the things that you don't know.

I use a risk communication tool quite a bit when I have to ski conservative terrain because of a lack confidence in my knowledge of say a persistent weak layer. I just say to them "You know what, I don't know exactly where it is, and I don't think you wanna be caught in a size 3 avalanche, so the only way I know how to manage this is to ski these low angle slopes." Total transparency around what we know and what we don't know.

When I teach people about standing back from a map to look at the big picture, it didn't escape me that that was a metaphor for so much of decision making - that standing back and getting the bigger picture.

When in doubt, you have to ask yourself foundational questions.

The primary goal every day is everyone ending the day safely.

End of the Expert's Reflections

What are the five key points you developed?

Key Points Generated by ChatGPT-4

Note: OpenAI has attached the following to its webpage "ChatGPT can make mistakes. Check important info." Do you agree with what has been summarized?

Big Picture Planning and Weather Interpretation:

Stand back from the map to get a macro view of the terrain and visualize how the weather, particularly a southwesterly flow, will interact with the terrain.

Use isobar lines and weather models to predict wind patterns and potential areas where visibility may be better or worse.

Observe current weather conditions directly by stepping outside, feeling the wind, and watching cloud movements to corroborate weather data.

Continuous Observation and Adaptation:

Keep your senses engaged throughout the day, constantly gathering information about wind direction and speed from the pilot and visual cues on the snow.

Be ready to adapt your plans based on real-time observations and feedback, verifying or refuting initial hypotheses about snow conditions and wind effects.

Conservative Terrain Selection:

When uncertainty about conditions, such as the presence of a persistent weak layer (PWL), is high, choose conservative terrain that minimizes risk.

Gradually expand to more challenging terrain only as confidence in conditions increases, collecting data through snow profiles and observing nearby areas for signs of stability.

Effective Communication with the Pilot:

Engage in thorough discussions with the pilot about visibility and landing safety before and during the flight.

Make decisions collaboratively, ensuring that both the guide's assessment of ski hazards and the pilot's requirements for safe landing and takeoff are met.

Client Communication and Risk Management:

Communicate openly with clients about safety priorities, especially when conservative terrain is chosen due to uncertain conditions.

Emphasize the importance of safety over the thrill of skiing more dangerous slopes, ensuring clients understand the rationale behind your decisions.

Use transparency to build trust, explaining what is known and unknown about snow conditions and how that informs terrain choices.

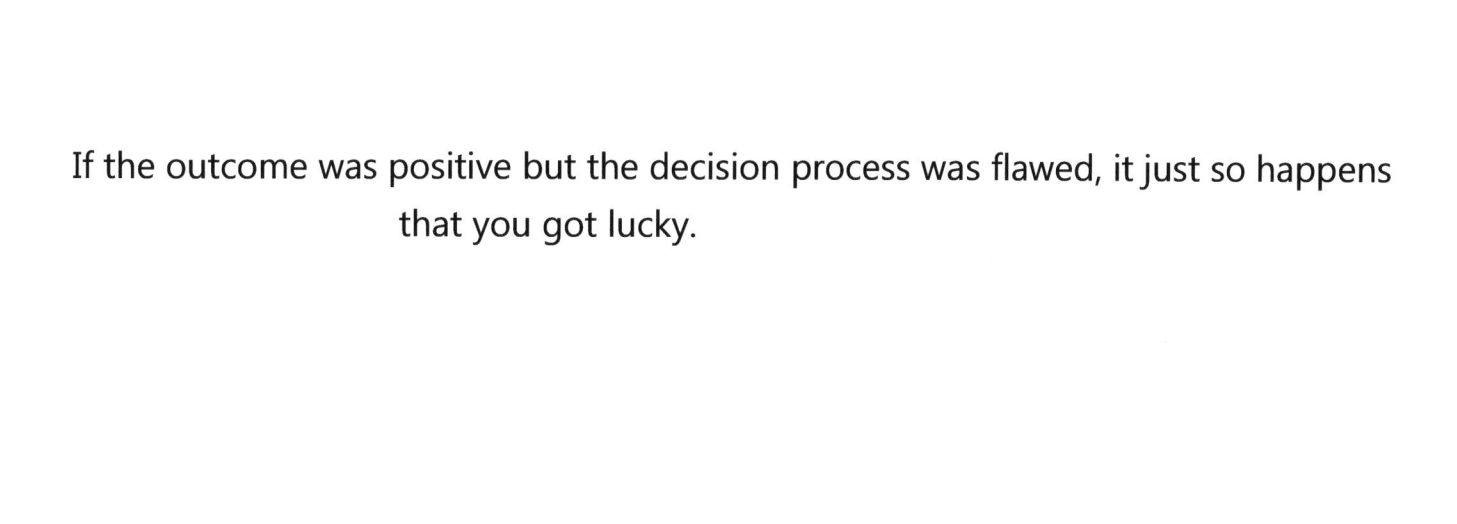

If the outcome was positive but the decision process was flawed, it just so happens that you got lucky.

Go Fetch - Balancing Avalanche Risk and Productivity

Read the following scenario developed from an interview with an expert and stop at the decision point question as indicated by the statement...

"Write down your cues, goals, and what are you thinking/doing."

The following is very important and is how you will learn using this method.

Put yourself in the place of the expert and write down what you would be thinking and or doing if you were in that situation. **If you don't take the time to do this... you won't learn.**

Note that the information in the scenario might be incomplete, much the same as it would be in the real world.

<u>Do not skip ahead</u>. Reading ahead to see what the expert has done before you have put your thoughts down, will negate the value of this exercise.

After you have put your thoughts on paper refer to the next page "Thoughts of the Expert...". Have you differed or missed something? Think about that.

Continue reading the scenario sections, writing down your thoughts, and reading those of the expert until you come to the end. Reflect about the situation. In the same position, would you make the same decisions? What would be the outcome of those decisions?

Read the Expert's reflections to gain context and deeper understanding.

During your review of the expert's scenario and their thoughts, write down 5 key points. Compare your 5 to those developed by ChatGPT-4.

If you have any questions or comments, please reach out to
helicourse@gmail.com

Go Fetch 1

After lots of experience in the backcountry you are now assigned to a major construction project in the Coast Mountains of BC as an avalanche tech. Your job is to keep the worksite safe and operating, mitigating the avalanche hazard throughout the winter. The prime contractor has just changed and is unfamiliar with the area and it's avalanche hazards. You have been there since early October watching the snowpack develop and accumulate. It is now mid-November, and a system is forecast to come through. The construction work is in full swing in the alpine with over a dozen excavators, numerous rock trucks, dozers, and pickup trucks on the large and spread out site. The goal is to reach a construction benchmark by having a certain amount of work done over the next two weeks.

You are based in a camp in the valley about 30 kilometres from the work site and have a remote sensing weather station a further 20 kilometres down valley. You have internet access. You need to make decisions about whether to keep the site open or not. You feel you have a reasonable handle on the snowpack data in the vicinity of the worksite which includes snow in the fetches, faceting, moraines, and inaccessible cliff bands. You have to make decisions about how to enable the contractor to get the work done and keep everyone safe.

(1). Write down your cues, goals, and what are you thinking/doing.

<u>Do not skip ahead.</u>

Thoughts and Actions of the Expert 1

We had specific zones where we limited the amount of machinery that could work there. There was another zone that was more of a transport area where they could move material to.

We tried to limit the exposure by only placing a few excavators in the really dangerous places. The mass of people, all your different people, your first aiders and all those kinds of people - we had them park well out of the line of fire so to speak, out of the runout zones.

First decision is "Do we have the window to even keep it open?" With the front coming, how are we are we managing it now that it's open and then what are the biggest factors.

Go Fetch 2

You go online and look at the weather using the GFA from NavCanada, Environment Canada's GEM Regional model, and the US National Weather Service NAM model to get a provincial sized understanding of the developing weather, the Avalanche Canada 5 day for more in depth snow forecasts and you also look at AlpineFX with customized local weather.

Yesterday you took the 40 minute drive up to the worksite and assessed the wind, snow depths, and loading at that time. There are areas of cliffy unskiable terrain and lower moraine features above the work site. The fetches have snow in them. The wind was light.

The information that you have gathered gives you an idea about the incoming front, it's size and timing, and the weather it will bring.

(2). Write down your cues, goals, and what are you thinking/doing.

Do not skip ahead.

Thoughts and Actions of the Expert 2

To add some layers of safety and some more confidence to the decision to keep the work going, we decided to be on site versus just forecasting it from camp and calling it a day.

Go Fetch 3

You head up in the morning a little bit behind the morning crews that went up super early. The plan is to have it open for the whole day. You are a couple of hours after them. As you are driving up, you quickly realize that the weather was significantly stronger than expected, so more wind and more precipitation. Essentially the front had arrived along earlier than you have anticipated. You are 25 kilometres into your 30 kilometre drive to get to the site up the FSR (forest service road) and there is a radio call "Avalanche!" from that work zone.

(3). Write down your cues, goals, and what are you thinking/doing.

<u>Do not skip ahead.</u>

Thoughts and Actions of the Expert 3

We get on the radio and figure out that there's been a natural avalanche that slid into the work zone, covered a large excavator up over its tracks and partway up the operator door.

Then, over the radio, we told everybody that they needed to leave the area back away and move down the road to the muster area.

The wind for whatever reason was there a number of hours before forecast, so that rapid loading was happening in the wee hours of the morning. We were anticipating it to pick up much later, at the end of the day. So, my margin was quite small in retrospect. I was relying on that loading to not have happened and it was already in process as we were driving up. I think if I had arrived earlier (ahead of the crew) to get that weather information I would've been like "Oh geez it's already honking windy here. Maybe I don't want to have people up here."

The reason it slid was rapid loading from the fetches onto early season faceting in really steep unskiable terrain, so really cliffy terrain. Those slides that were naturally triggering were triggering not smaller, but slab avalanches that were on moraine features that the machines were underneath. That was our best deduction of what was triggering the cycle. Nothing to anchor the slopes and just rapid loading.

So, nobody got hurt, nothing got broken, but they ended up not getting the work done. It took another 3 or 4 days before we could really get in there, do control and make the area safe.

End of Scenario

The Expert's Reflections ...

I didn't have the sort of working relationship totally dialed yet with those guys. We weren't at that comfortable stage with any of those contractors. We were still figuring each other out and classically I was aiming to please. Anything in the moment seemed reasonable.

I think my actual experience may have been the very thing that pushed me into like being OK with having a smaller margin. I think somebody who wasn't used to being on the Coast may have may have given themselves a larger margin. Finding that balance between productivity and safety is so important but so tricky and nuanced.

A D8 cat broke down and had to be left behind when we evacuated the site after the size 2 hit the excavator. It turned out to be a really big avalanche cycle in the end when that storm peaked, so we had cut it pretty close.

We had to leave the cat there and once they saw the results of the avalanche control mission in relation to their D8 that effectively got buried, they then kind of went like "Oh this is a big deal". That's when we started to get buy in from them. They literally opened the bank account to our explosive control program, like whatever it costs, just keep your mag full. So once they kind of understood the hazard, that's when we really started building that relationship of, we're not just writing a bulletin, we're actually physically changing your work site to make it safe.

The not knowing exactly where the contractor sort of risk acceptability level is or was, that is an unknown.

A great strategy I learned out of this was and that I would apply later if I was to do this again would be come at it from "Hey we can do this for you." We can do the work and here are your options. So, I started spelling out for them "Here's option A, option B, option C. A is expensive it's gonna take time it's going to be effective. Option B is more expensive. Option C, the margin of error is a little bit smaller, it's going to take longer but it's going to be cheap."

So basically, you're laying all these options for them and then they make the choice which in turn for removes the operational pressure from me. Then I'm not the one saying, "I can have this open for you in 24 hours". It's them picking and saying "We want you to do this" (at your consultation of course) but we the customer choose this. Then I can say, "OK I can work with that, if that's what you want."

Some really good things came out of it too in in the end. I basically went to them and said "Look we need weather stations. If we're always having to go to site to get weather, we spend a lot of time and resources doing that. We come back to the office and make decisions with "old" data and put out the bulletin. But if we have weather stations, we get the data in real time. I can be up at 2:00 in the morning looking at this stuff. Our effectiveness can be increased in terms of putting out an accurate bulletin and increasing safety because we can make good decisions with good data."

So, we brought them a proposal for weather stations. It was crazy expensive, and they didn't even blink because they did the math of the cost of the weather stations versus that of a delayed job. They said go ahead and install them and that's how we end up getting those four stations over on the project.

In a similar situation I think a novice might have gotten steamrolled by the contractor. I think the novice would have gotten pushed because the novice wouldn't have had the assertiveness and the (I don't know what the right word is, backbone?) to sort of keep the game going. I think they would have gotten pushed even after an avalanche.

Do I think a novice would recognize that? Sure, there's been one avalanche, but would they recognize that there could be more or that or was that just the only one? It's important to have an understanding the scope of the terrain that's above them and how it all interacts. There's so much nuance that goes into that that even at the expert level, when you're given that clue, you don't have to think about the nuance anymore it's like, we have the clue. We're good. We're done.

We were knowingly pushing a little bit. So, to answer the question what would I have told my replacement if I had to leave the night before? I know I don't appreciate walking into a scenario with somebody handing it off to me and saying, "Hey man, here's the freaking bomb, the fuse is lit but you should be good till 4:00 PM. Hopefully you can get it cleared out." When you put it that way it just sounds ridiculous. Why were you even there?

When there's the option to make that easy decision, then you should take it.

End of the Expert's Reflections

What are the five key points you developed?

Key Points Generated by ChatGPT-4

Note: OpenAI has attached the following to its webpage "ChatGPT can make mistakes. Check important info." Do you agree with what has been summarized?

Prioritize Safety with Detailed Risk Assessments:

Continuously monitor weather forecasts and snowpack conditions using multiple sources to stay informed about potential avalanche risks.

Perform on-site assessments early and regularly to verify the conditions, especially before the crew arrives. Be prepared to adapt plans based on real-time observations.

Implement Zoning and Limit Exposure:

Designate specific zones for different levels of machinery operation to limit the number of high-risk areas exposed at any time. Ensure that high-exposure zones have minimal machinery and personnel.

Establish clear muster areas away from runout zones for all non-essential personnel to ensure their safety during high-risk periods.

Effective Communication and Decision Making:

Clearly communicate avalanche risks and safety protocols to the construction team, especially when unexpected weather conditions arise. Make sure everyone knows the evacuation plan and the importance of adhering to safety zones.

Involve the contractor in decision-making by presenting various safety and operational options to ensure they understand and support safety priorities.

Maintain Robust Relationships and Assertiveness:

Develop a strong working relationship with the contractor by demonstrating the importance of safety measures and their impact on overall project success. Use past incidents (the buried excavator) to illustrate hazards and the need for safety protocols.

Stand firm on safety decisions, even if it means delaying work. Do not compromise on margins of safety to meet deadlines, and ensure that all decisions are made with a clear understanding of the risks involved.

Leverage Technology for Enhanced Safety:

Advocate for the installation of remote weather stations to obtain real-time data, which enhances decision-making and reduces the need for constant on-site assessments.

Use this data to provide accurate and timely safety bulletins, improving overall project safety and efficiency by making informed decisions based on up-to-date information.

"

Amateurs have a goal. Professionals have a system.

Pockets and Pipes - Balancing Risk, Responsibility, and Thrill

Read the following scenario developed from an interview with an expert and stop at the decision point question as indicated by the statement...

"Write down your cues, goals, and what are you thinking/doing."

The following is very important and is how you will learn using this method.

Put yourself in the place of the expert and write down what you would be thinking and or doing if you were in that situation. **If you don't take the time to do this... you won't learn.**

Note that the information in the scenario might be incomplete, much the same as it would be in the real world.

<u>Do not skip ahead</u>. Reading ahead to see what the expert has done before you have put your thoughts down, will negate the value of this exercise.

After you have put your thoughts on paper refer to the next page "Thoughts of the Expert...". Have you differed or missed something? Think about that.

Continue reading the scenario sections, writing down your thoughts, and reading those of the expert until you come to the end. Reflect about the situation. In the same position, would you make the same decisions? What would be the outcome of those decisions?

Read the Expert's reflections to gain context and deeper understanding.

During your review of the expert's scenario and their thoughts, write down 5 key points. Compare your 5 to those developed by ChatGPT-4.

If you have any questions or comments, please reach out to
helicourse@gmail.com

Your willingness to believe something is influenced by how much you want and need it to be true.

Pockets and Pipes 1

You are the heliski operations manager with responsibility for the entire multi machine operation. Today you are flying with a private group of 3, two snowboarders and a skier. The snowpack is unstable, made up of three surface hoar layers in the top 70 centimeters with no recent fresh snow.

Your morning has the added pressure of a delayed start. You have to take a helicopter to a nearby backcountry lodge and inform the locals there to return to town because of the recent avalanche death of a mutual friend.

After the late start and only a couple of runs in, a call comes over the radio from another private group of an avalanche involvement on the run called Alpha, 40 kilometres away. You take your group, fly across the mountain range and end up being first on the scene, landing in the meadow below Alpha, just as the person was found.

In order to safely ski Alpha, the guide had specifically told his private group to stay on the ridge. One of the guests had veered off this ridge line causing a slide at which point the pilot, waiting in the helicopter parked below, had called up on the radio and said there's an avalanche. The guest did not show up when the guide had regrouped below, so the instant thought was that this guest had been the trigger and was in the avalanche. Turns out they had triggered it but weren't in the slide. As they had lost a ski, it takes a bit of time to get everything sorted out.

You have gone from skiing way over there and have come across the range in a 20 minute flight, ending up in this new place. You know this area really well but still, it is kind of a big left-hander from your original plan for the day and where you were going to ski.

You have been skiing tracks all week because it hasn't snowed for a while and so you are still looking for those little pockets of fresh snow.

The guests in your private group include a prominent businessman who is really nice but eager to get after it and to ski hard. He says "OK, we've been just kinda deviated about 20 minutes. We use my heli time for this, my heli time for that, and now how about let's go? I wanna ski. Let's get on with the day here."

(1). Write down your cues, goals, and what are you thinking/doing.

<u>Do not skip ahead.</u>

Thoughts and Actions of the Expert 1

We need to get skiing as quickly as possible.

Alpha is not somewhere that I would have chosen to go. I could have skied it but I would have to work hard to keep everybody together and safe, as was just proven.

I thought I've got this big beautiful run beside us, over here at Zulu. I can go and do that, it's a much easier choice.

Zulu is right next to Alpha and is a run that has perfectly safe conditions without any risk of avalanches, as long as you choose the right line. So I thought Zulu was a good place to go and get started again.

The pressure wasn't so much about the ski quality as it was the dynamics of the day, to get the day moving forward in a positive light. We have all these stressful negative type things happen in the morning that I was really connected to, but the clients weren't. To them, it was just delays along the way. I think the pressure that I felt was to provide a product and to get everything flowing in a positive way.

Pockets and Pipes 2

You fly around the corner to the beautiful run called Zulu. It's this big open slope. There's some glacier on the top but it has receded and made these big long ramps, interspersed with gullies that can hold four to six people. These gullies are perfect natural half pipes. They are consecutive across the run and there are no tracks over there.

Zulu

To the left is a large unskiable bowl. You can stay completely away from any avalanche risk on Zulu by going far over to the right, but then you come out at the bottom where there's a traverse and a flatter runout. Going this way would make the snowboarders walk to get to the helicopter pick up.

Leaving the top, you make a decision to drop in a bit earlier above the half pipes which is still on safe terrain. I tell the clients to ski left or right of my tracks for the first pitch as it was just a planar mellow slope.

Finally the day starts to flow, you find that the skiing is amazing, beautiful snow. The clients are experts skiers and Zulu (marked) is right in their wheelhouse where they can rip from top to bottom. They certainly can do it and the skiing is great. You come to the start of the ribs and half pipes (marked).

Typical Pipes

(2). Write down your cues, goals, and what are you thinking/doing.

Do not skip ahead.

Thoughts and Actions of the Expert 2

In my head I was "I don't want to stop, this is so good". As I was skiing I was thinking "Should I? Shouldn't I? Should I? Shouldn't I?" Do I need to worry about being too cautious by stopping and interrupting a great run?

I thought I'd better stop and regroup but in my head I was thinking "I don't want to stop as the skiing is so good and the day is starting to flow. But I had better stop because even though we have just seen this avalanche, there is potential for involvement and I bet if I don't stop someone's probably going to go into this halfpipe."

The ridge was wide enough that it would be a deviation for the guests to go into the half pipe – that was my challenge, because the ridge was the obvious place to ski but the half pipes would look like fun so if I stopped and interrupted the flow to tell them something they weren't going to do anyway, it would be a bummer. But I couldn't take the chance they might be tempted to deviate from where I was going. The half pipes were a change in terrain but not so far away from my line that it might not be obvious to them.

I stop above the halfpipes at the first blue x and wait for the clients. I said "OK we're going to stay right on this ridge here. We don't want to go down into these gullies, we could trigger something. So, we're just going stay on the ridge and go along where there's lots of room."

After I explain that to them, the client said, "Well it's a good thing you stopped here because we were gonna go straight for that that gully. That's a perfect half pipe, it looks so good. I'm not going to now, but it's a good thing you stopped here to tell me because otherwise I would've been in there for sure."

We ski down the rib and come out onto this nice flat bench. I'm pulling up to a stop (second blue x) when I see this ton of snow go whooshing down beside me, just below the ridge, only 20 meters away. I looked up and there are the two snowboarders right behind me, stopped. The avalanche is coming down one of the gullies.

The skier had done something, like cross his tips or whatever, fell and lost a ski. It went right in on the side of the gully. He didn't go into the gully at all, but the ski alone did cause a skier remote, a full size 2. That was the avalanche that was coming down past us. I looked back up to see where he was. He was OK, picking up his ski and putting it back on.

He comes down and we talked about how lucky it was that we had stopped and talked about staying on the ridges. They would have gone into the gully for sure and then we see the avalanche and they say "OK yeah, this is something to pay attention to and we're going to listen to you and all of your instructions."

End of Scenario

The Expert's Reflections ...

The avalanche conditions that winter grew to be historic with size 3 avalanches running out into 18° terrain. Creeks would fracture and turn into slides size 2 1/2 because the snow would just pile up. There were huge avalanches from places where you think that maybe you could barely get a size 1 out of them, but the propagation was so massive.

I don't think the very experienced guides understood the magnitude of it as early as we did because they had maybe a few more options, more mellow places to go. I think they also thought they could figure it out a little bit more. One or two guides I think pushed into some bigger terrain and didn't have anything happen, giving that type of feedback to them. At that point, those were not the places that I would have chosen to go. The younger guides seemed to back off a little bit sooner. The older ones seemed to have a bit more confidence early on because they thought they could out think the avalanche problem. That changed when one had a skier remote size 3 about 10' from their feet.

I had been setting my brain up to respond to an avalanche with someone buried, mentally preparing for that. I would have been preoccupied with all the things that I was going to call for, and how it was going to operate logistically.

Then it switches instantly to OK, everything is good, let's go back skiing.

I think subconsciously I knew I was going to stay out of the half pipes but I didn't think about it too much until I started skiing. I was processing the events that had just happened, the terrain, the reason, and the fact that there's probably the same issue here with the layers.

So I was processing as I was skiing down off the top through the nice mellow terrain. I was thinking through the process, what am I doing, where am I going, and who do I have following me? All these things were going through my head.

Without the precursor of the other private group's avalanche, I probably wouldn't have stopped where I did and told the clients to stay out of the gullies. I don't know if that decision was because the layers were there. They didn't become reactive for a little while. It took some time for them to kind of set up and actually start showing any kind of instability. Surface hoar will sit and there won't be any tension. Then somewhere in there, usually 17 to 21 days afterwards, it tends to get a little bit more cohesion from settling and you start seeing reactivity from it. I think the decision to stop and brief the clients was definitely influenced by the fact that we had just seen the sensitivity on Alpha which is right beside Zulu.

I think that if you didn't know any differently, you would just ski where ever you want. Those gullies are not menacing to look at but there is enough there at the perfect angle to create a terrain trap. They have a hollow bottom so if you get pushed in, the snow gets piled up on top of you, versus a planar slope where you just get pushed out the bottom and you can kind of stay more on the surface.

The more conservative choice would have been to come across right and take the line to the flatter runout but instead I skied where I did. It was a safe line but exposed on either side. I probably could have done a better job by just going way out to the right side and skiing the more mellow route. It would have been the easier, the better choice with no issues whatsoever. Now with my experience, I would choose to go right.

You want to find the line, to find the balance between fun exciting skiing and staying safe. You want to give yourself a margin of safety but you can take that too far. If you go and walk down places – very safe, but people won't come back and ski with you. If you go ski super gnarly and have incidents, then no one will ski with you either. So you have to find that balance in the middle, the area where you can accomplish both things, fun exciting skiing and staying safe.

Listen to your gut and act on it. I would say the three things to think about are, is there a gliding layer in the snowpack, is it an avalanche slope, and what are the consequences if it slides? Those are the kind of the three big ones - gliding layer, avalanche slope, and what are the consequences if you're wrong. I would say that you want to guide to the terrain or ski to the terrain, not the hazard rating. That means use your guiding procedures even when stability is good – in case your assessment is wrong!

I don't think people retain the goal of 'To come home safely' throughout a day. It gets lost in all the other influences of the day. I don't think "Am I getting home?" is a question that people ask very widely when they go out. They might ask it or think about it at the start but along the way they don't ask that question specifically. I think back to some of the accidents that have happened to people and it's just so sad because it's so seemingly obvious in hindsight how they got themselves in a bad situation. At the time they're distracted by other influences or oblivious to changing conditions.

I don't think people start to really realize the consequences that an accident can have until they have something happen to them or someone really close to them.

End of the Expert's Reflections

What are the five key points you developed?

Key Points Generated by ChatGPT-4

Note: OpenAI has attached the following to its webpage "ChatGPT can make mistakes. Check important info." Do you agree with what has been summarized?

Prioritize Immediate Safety and Clear Communication:

In any emergency situation, such as an avalanche involvement, immediately prioritize the safety of all parties. Ensure clear and direct communication with both the helicopter pilot and other guides to coordinate a rapid and effective response.

After ensuring the situation is safe, regroup and clearly communicate the plan and safety protocols to the guests, emphasizing the importance of staying on safe lines.

Adapt Plans Quickly Based on Real-Time Conditions:

Be prepared to adapt your skiing plans based on changing conditions and unforeseen events. When the original plan is disrupted (e.g., due to an avalanche on a nearby run), quickly assess alternative safe routes that still provide a good skiing experience.

Utilize your knowledge of the terrain to choose safer alternatives, like opting for Zulu over Alpha, to keep the day flowing smoothly while maintaining safety.

Balance Guest Expectations with Safety:

Manage the expectations of guests who may be eager to ski hard by balancing their desires with the need to keep them safe. Explain the reasons behind your decisions to help them understand the importance of sticking to safer terrain.

Ensure that your decisions prioritize safety without compromising the overall experience. Find the middle ground where guests can enjoy exciting skiing without taking unnecessary risks.

Continued...

Trust Your Instincts and Make Conservative Decisions:

When in doubt, trust your instincts and make conservative decisions. Stopping to regroup and inform clients about potential hazards, even when the skiing is good, is crucial to prevent incidents.

Regularly evaluate the snowpack and terrain for potential risks, considering factors like surface hoar layers and terrain traps, and adjust your plans accordingly to maintain a margin of safety.

Continuous Risk Assessment and Reflection:

Continuously assess the snowpack conditions, including identifying gliding layers and understanding the potential consequences of a slide. Use this ongoing assessment to guide your decisions throughout the day.

Reflect on your choices and outcomes to improve future decision-making. Learn from each experience, considering what could have been done differently to enhance safety while maintaining a positive experience for the guests.

Yes Boss - Confidence, Consequences, and Leadership Dynamics

Read the following scenario developed from an interview with an expert and stop at the decision point question as indicated by the statement...

"Write down your cues, goals, and what are you thinking/doing."

The following is very important and is how you will learn using this method.

Put yourself in the place of the expert and write down what you would be thinking and or doing if you were in that situation. **If you don't take the time to do this... you won't learn.**

Note that the information in the scenario might be incomplete, much the same as it would be in the real world.

<u>Do not skip ahead</u>. Reading ahead to see what the expert has done before you have put your thoughts down, will negate the value of this exercise.

After you have put your thoughts on paper refer to the next page "Thoughts of the Expert...". Have you differed or missed something? Think about that.

Continue reading the scenario sections, writing down your thoughts, and reading those of the expert until you come to the end. Reflect about the situation. In the same position, would you make the same decisions? What would be the outcome of those decisions?

Read the Expert's reflections to gain context and deeper understanding.

During your review of the expert's scenario and their thoughts, write down 5 key points. Compare your 5 to those developed by ChatGPT-4.

If you have any questions or comments, please reach out to
helicourse@gmail.com

Nothing is as persuasive as what you've experienced firsthand.

Yes Boss 1

You are relatively new to the industry and are working as an avalanche tech at a large Rocky Mountain ski resort. You and your team leader have been sent out as a pair, as is the standard operating procedure, to do control work opening up closed terrain.

It is late in the ski day, and you've been on a regular control route. There are still some areas to do but in your mind it doesn't matter if it gets done immediately. Even if you get this run opened, it is so late in the day the skiers wouldn't be able to access it and make the last chair. You have used all your hand charges, so you are traveling with just your packs.

Zulu is a treeless run in high alpine terrain with a rollover into a cornice, then a wide open slope down onto the flats. It isn't one that runs frequently. It builds on the big and fat short slope finishing into a low angle landing. The last storm has cross loaded it, leaving it ripe for avalanches. You ski over towards the top of Zulu and your team leader, standing away from you on the rollover says, "We're going to ski cut this." You are uneasy about that plan because you feel the position where he has stopped and the slope as a whole is too dangerous, ready to slide.

(1). Write down your cues, goals, and what are you thinking/doing.

<u>Do not skip ahead</u>

Thoughts and Actions of the Expert 1

There's no pressure from the ski area. It's really late in the day and I'm thinking this is crazy. As he goes to the rollover I called to him and said, "You're not in a safe spot." He said "I'm the team leader. This is a safe spot. It won't pull out. Look at this little tree beside me."

Yes Boss 2

The team lead calls to you saying "Come on over here and we're going to talk about what we do." So you go over to where he is standing and he says "I want you to get over this roll and ski along under the cornice. Work the rolls over at the far end then ski back up on top."

Then he said "Don't worry. There's not a problem, you go first."

(2). Write down your cues, goals, and what are you thinking/doing.

<u>Do not skip ahead</u>

Thoughts and Actions of the Expert 2

I didn't have the confidence to say "Look I can't do this. Let's do a different approach or come back tomorrow or discuss it with the commander-in-chief." I had learned a little bit and there's some common sense involved here. I didn't have a great deal of trust in my team leader, and it may have been because of my inexperience or just my relationship with him. I'm not sure what was happening there.

Again, that lack of confidence, that'll make you do things. The confidence in my reasoning wasn't strong. I wasn't able to counter his plan because I wasn't sure if my ideas would be challenged, or I didn't know how strongly I believed in them.

We could've waited till the next day and tested it with explosives.

It is not to say the junior guy doesn't have a valid opinion but we tend to look to the experts. And the experts are people that have more experience, right? They have been exposed to more situations and we're trusting that.

In the early morning when you're trying to open the slopes and people are waiting there, waiting for the open signs, there's a little more pressure. You're asked "How quickly are you guys working, what steps are you taking, are you sure you can't get by with one bomb and one ski cut?" This list of pressures exists but later in the day, there wasn't any time pressure. We didn't need to be there.

So I started to side slip down over this roll to get under the cornice. I zipped across and got about 90% of the way across to where I was just going to ascend up back on top of the cornice.

At that moment the whole slope released including where he was standing, the spot that I had said was unsafe. I'm not sure why I had been worried about that spot, maybe it was intuition. We both got carried down and hit a lake with enough force that we broke the ice. I lost some gear there. It's probably at lake bottom.

You know you have a fracture line at the cornice called the crown? At the bottom it's called the stauchwall. When we were going down, I could feel myself hit that. I was getting buried, and the stauchwall popped me out of the snow. When we stopped, I was kind of buried to the waist and I could dig myself out. Some of our teammates were up on top of the mountain and they were looking down and reported it right away, but we were out, we were OK. It was close to being a deadly event.

End of Scenario

The Expert's Reflections ...

So that's an incident I was involved in. Did I have a positive effect on it? No, because I didn't have the confidence at that time. I think for a lot of people if you're out skiing in a group and you've got some knowledge, it's really hard to be the guy that says "Let's turn around, I don't want to ski this slope."

When you're new, you're counting on the leaders to guide you. You're with people all the time that have experience and knowledge. It's not just you relying on yourself. Later, the more you learn, the more you contribute to the decision that will be acceptable to you.

Initially I would rely somewhat on the team leader to make a decision. I may doubt that decision, but I didn't have as much experience as them and I might have had a hard time articulating why I wasn't feeling good about a decision made by someone else. Later on you have more confidence in your decision making, you've got more experience, and your voice is stronger. You have an opinion on where you should go and where you shouldn't be.

It's harder to turn around when you're new at the game because you could say, "Well that doesn't feel good to me", but you can't tell people why. With experience, you could be talking to them about how the snowpack built through the year and we've had bigger loading, temperatures are rising, the buried layer isn't changing, all of those things. The more experience you have, the more confidence you gain, so you feel more capable of expressing your opinion.

I didn't really trust him because of his decision making abilities. I had been with him before and had seen him make previous decisions. That was his last year there by the way, because of incidents like that. I thought it was a poor call going in there without bombs and also putting ourselves onto a potentially risky slope. I just didn't feel the decision making was good at that time and you learn from that.

There's a lot of personality stuff involved as well, it's not all about avalanche knowledge. Some of it is do you trust people? Are they easy to work with or are they a pain in the ***? I think if I had been involved longer in the job and had more confidence in expressing myself, we could have avoided that incident. I would have been a different person, one who speaks out.

This happens in ski touring as well I think - egos. Especially when it is inexperienced people in a bunch of macho guys out there. Something in the egos, not wanting to back out, plays a role in who dies and who lives.

Once when I was touring I did a little ski cut at the top and I said "You know, I had an experience with snow that felt this way. When I had got down to the bottom of the run and skied off the slab, everything went. I'm not comfortable in here." So I said, "Guys, it is likely this isn't going to slide. We're probably not going to hit the trigger. We can ski this, but I'm feeling a little uncomfortable. The consequences of this sliding at this time of the day is one of us isn't going home." So we turned around and went down the way we came up.

Another young guy came up by himself and skied that slope. We were in the bar afterwards and he's in there talking about how great it was. We had turned it down. I thought about that a lot. I thought I was doing what I wanted to do. I was happy with that decision.

So, if I was teaching a course I would tell the people, go with the weakest person in your group. If anybody wants to turn around, just go with that. Good decisions ensure you're still around for a lot of good skiing in the future.

That's the other thing that's been important for me is choosing the people you ski with. There are some Yahoo skiers around who say "Let's go touring together!" but they are caught in slides lots and so I reply "Yeah that would be fun. I'd like to go with you but I'm busy tomorrow" or whatever.

Choose who you're going to be with. It's even choosing what are those people like to talk with? What is it like to be with them? Do they respect your decisions or would they be pressuring you? You should have criteria for picking who you spend time with.

We were taught only one person is ever exposed. I would never have a whole group on a slope at once. So most of my touring has been with two other guys. All of us have the same attitude, same risk tolerance.

I'm surprised that quite often a whole group is exposed and how the communication isn't hitting the back of the ski touring line. I've often been in the middle of the line going up and said to the people "You know this whole slope hasn't gone with the first five of guys across so it is not going to go, but let's just practice good habits here and spread out. It seems that once it is said, everybody buys into the idea and says, "Yeah, let's do that".

Once you are spread out crossing this slope the second last guy should be spotting the last guy because the last guy could disappear trying to catch up to the rest of group. Actually, once our group got really spread out. I was up front with the guide and a slide came down between the last guys and us. They had to go over the debris. What are the chances?

At this point in my life, I realize you don't make mistakes late in the day.

So, it's funny, that stuff brings up emotions now and what was that; 40 years ago?

Sometimes you have to miss a lot of good skiing so that you can have a life long enough to enjoy a lot of skiing. It's not like you're missing that one run, you're ensuring you're around for a life of runs.

End of the Expert's Reflections

What are the five key points you developed?

Key Points Generated by ChatGPT-4

Note: OpenAI has attached the following to its webpage "ChatGPT can make mistakes. Check important info." Do you agree with what has been summarized?

Trust Your Instincts and Speak Up:

Always trust your gut feelings and speak up if you sense danger. Even as a novice, your concerns are valid and can prevent accidents. Confidence in your judgment is crucial for safety.

Assess the Necessity of the Task:

Evaluate whether the task is essential, especially under non-urgent conditions. In this scenario, opening the run late in the day wasn't necessary. Prioritize tasks based on the urgency and potential risks involved.

Understand and Respect Terrain and Snowpack Conditions:

Continuously assess the terrain and snowpack. Recognize factors like cross-loading and instability that could trigger avalanches. Make decisions based on a thorough understanding of the snowpack's behavior and potential risks.

Minimize Exposure and Maintain Clear Communication:

Ensure that only one person is exposed to potential hazards at a time. Maintain clear and consistent communication within the team. Respect each other's safety concerns and work together to make informed decisions.

Learn from Experience and Build Confidence:

Learn from past incidents and experiences. Building experience over time enhances your decision-making abilities and confidence. As you gain more knowledge, your input will become more valuable and respected in team decisions.

In heliski you change your terrain. In avalanche control you get rid of the danger.

Bada Boom - Strategic Avalanche Control Amid Pressure

Read the following scenario developed from an interview with an expert and stop at the decision point question as indicated by the statement...

"Write down your cues, goals, and what are you thinking/doing."

The following is very important and is how you will learn using this method.

Put yourself in the place of the expert and write down what you would be thinking and or doing if you were in that situation. **If you don't take the time to do this... you won't learn.**

Note that the information in the scenario might be incomplete, much the same as it would be in the real world.

Do not skip ahead. Reading ahead to see what the expert has done before you have put your thoughts down, will negate the value of this exercise.

After you have put your thoughts on paper refer to the next page "Thoughts of the Expert...". Have you differed or missed something? Think about that.

Continue reading the scenario sections, writing down your thoughts, and reading those of the expert until you come to the end. Reflect about the situation. In the same position, would you make the same decisions? What would be the outcome of those decisions?

Read the Expert's reflections to gain context and deeper understanding.

During your review of the expert's scenario and their thoughts, write down 5 key points. Compare your 5 to those developed by ChatGPT-4.

If you have any questions or comments, please reach out to
helicourse@gmail.com

Bada Boom 1

You are working as an avalanche control technician in the Coast Mountains on a major project. The project has been ongoing for two years and is a big spend (eventually surpassing $500 million) with a mandate of zero accidents that is fully supported by the management. However slowing the job down is not an option. The pressure to keep the work going is real.

Your job is to protect the road up the valley to the worksite. It is tiger country with 2000 metre high mountains towering over the road and numerous avalanche paths running full length down to the valley. The average snow fall is over 5 metres and this year has been above average. As in most coastal snowpacks, there is a deeply buried and nasty persistent weak layer (PWL). You and your assistant have at your disposal a helicopter, are trained in the use of avalanche explosives, and have been using both in trying to keep the overhead hazard to a minimum by repeatedly bringing down small avalanches.

A major storm has just past through leaving yet more snow on top of the PWL and large cornices overhanging the road. The weather window to fly is open for a short while before the next front moves in.

(1). Write down your cues, goals, and what are you thinking/doing.
<u>Do not skip ahead</u>

Thoughts and Actions of the Expert 1

Working safely and keeping the road open are not necessarily mutually exclusive.

When the weather is non flyable get everything ready for the weather window i.e. explosives, helicopter, communication, personnel for road closure and control, equipment and personnel for opening road.

Confirm the weather forecasts. Confirm length of weather window for control work. Confirm timing for next storm. Confirm expected loading and loading rate in the next forecasted storm. Review temperature forecast. Review forecast winds.

Review the snowpack data. Review the slide path data which refers to the daily records of all slide paths, when they ran, if they ran full path, how complete was cleanup and what is still hanging on slide path.

Gather more info, snow profiles to identify weak layer, coastal snowpacks/equivalent temp, is rapid change likely?

Know your terrain. Identify the target zones that will provide best results. Identify slopes most likely to self stabilize in next storm cycle. Are there big fetch areas on the windward side of your controlled zones or high ridges that act as a snow fence. What is around you that will affect loading in your area?

Determine the best approach to get the load on the slope that will reach the buried weak layer i.e. cornice blasting, heli bombing, type and size of explosive.

If we were using guns, make sure the ammo and coordinates are in place.

Develop a contingency plan. What if the weather window disappears? Be prepared to protect personal and infrastructure.

Road openings may be short lived. All the road users should be kept informed of pending closings and openings. Communicate that all traffic should be ready to roll when safe and plan on moving quickly while the opportunity exists.

Load up and do da damage!

End of Scenario

The Expert's Reflections ...

Avi control is; think ahead, be prepared, double check.

An Avi forecasters job is easiest when the hazard is extreme or low but spookiest when the hazard is in the middle at considerable.

If you have a persistent weak layer (PWL) in heliskiing, it's my understanding that you change your terrain to stay safe. In avalanche control you get rid of the danger. If you have to put a bigger bomb in there, have to dig more holes, if you have to do ski cuts or whatever it is, you stabilize that slope. Ski guides are not going to say "Well, let's stop and stabilize this slope".

I was a big fan of fast burning explosives and lots of them. I wasn't a fan of Amex, as it burns at 3000 meters a second and where I was using it, it doesn't give enough punch to the snow. Some people said it gives a push. I never believed that was effective but then there was lots of debate in the scientific papers on it back then. So I was buying a thing called Powerfrac. It burned at 6100 meters per second so with double the burn rate, it gave a lot of punch.

If you throw a bomb onto the surface looking to take out a weakness that is deeper down in the snow pack, you might also have a surface weakness. If that explosion triggers the surface, it is questionable if you have enough mass sliding to step down and take out the buried layer. I just thought "What we need is to have this road open, it needs to be safe, our weather window is not very frequent. Let's put a big bomb on there. If there is any weakness, let's find it"

Ski resorts are cheap but at the big job sites, I could burn up all explosives I wanted to. I would knock the huge cornices off onto the slope, the huge mass of sliding snow getting at that deep PWL. So, we flew up net loads of explosives (hundreds of kilograms) and instead of putting one kilogram charges on a cornice, I put boxes with primed charges and then I tied them altogether with a trunk line. We got spectacular huge slides filling creeks and valleys and then up, up the other side over the road and up through the trees. We didn't have a hazard there for long.

Our goal was to get the snow out frequently enough that the road didn't get buried. We wanted to have the road open so people could just drive up and do their work. While the size 4 deeply burying the road was spectacular and got the avalanche danger message across to the client, it was not excellent control work. Ideally we wanted to bring the snow down without it crossing and closing the road.

End of the Expert's Reflections

What are the five key points you developed?

Key Points Generated by ChatGPT-4

Note: OpenAI has attached the following to its webpage "ChatGPT can make mistakes. Check important info." Do you agree with what has been summarized?

Preparation and Readiness for Short Weather Windows:

Ensure all equipment, personnel, and plans are ready before the weather window opens. This includes explosives, helicopters, communication systems, road closure protocols, and road opening crews.

Confirm the latest weather forecasts, including the duration of the window and details about the upcoming storm, such as expected loading rates, temperature changes, and wind conditions.

Comprehensive Snowpack and Terrain Analysis:

Continuously review snowpack data and slide path records. Assess which slopes are most likely to release and which might stabilize on their own.

Gather additional information through snow profiles to identify the persistent weak layer (PWL) and consider the coastal snowpack characteristics to anticipate rapid changes.

Effective Use of Explosives for Hazard Mitigation:

Determine the best method to reach and destabilize the buried weak layer, such as cornice blasting or heli-bombing, and choose appropriate explosives (e.g., high-velocity Powerfrac over Amex).

Employ large charges to ensure deep-layer weaknesses are addressed, preventing partial releases that could leave hazardous conditions intact.

Adaptive and Proactive Risk Management:

Develop contingency plans in case the weather window closes prematurely. Be ready to protect personnel and infrastructure if the situation changes suddenly.

Communicate clearly and frequently with all road users about pending closures and openings, ensuring they are prepared to move quickly when it is safe to do so.

Balancing Safety with Operational Demands:

Prioritize safety while acknowledging the need to keep the road open. This may involve frequent smaller avalanches rather than allowing large, dangerous buildups.

Aim to bring down snow in a controlled manner that minimizes road closures, ensuring the road is open as much as possible for the ongoing project.

"Novices fail to see the complexity that are apparent to a master. Masters see the simplicity hiding in complexity." Shane Parrish

What's for Launch? – Avalauncher Decisions: Navigating Instability Risks.

Read the following scenario developed from an interview with an expert and stop at the decision point question as indicated by the statement...

"Write down your cues, goals, and what are you thinking/doing."

The following is very important and is how you will learn using this method.

Put yourself in the place of the expert and write down what you would be thinking and or doing if you were in that situation. **If you don't take the time to do this... you won't learn.**

Note that the information in the scenario might be incomplete, much the same as it would be in the real world.

<u>Do not skip ahead</u>. Reading ahead to see what the expert has done before you have put your thoughts down, will negate the value of this exercise.

After you have put your thoughts on paper refer to the next page "Thoughts of the Expert...". Have you differed or missed something? Think about that.

Continue reading the scenario sections, writing down your thoughts, and reading those of the expert until you come to the end. Reflect about the situation. In the same position, would you make the same decisions? What would be the outcome of those decisions?

Read the Expert's reflections to gain context and deeper understanding.

During your review of the expert's scenario and their thoughts, write down 5 key points. Compare your 5 to those developed by ChatGPT-4.

If you have any questions or comments, please reach out to
helicourse@gmail.com

One of the things that you learn as you go is the greater your uncertainty, the greater your margin of safety has to be.

What's for Launch 1

You are a ski patroller at a Rocky Mountain ski resort. It is mid winter and there is the typical Rockies instability in the new snow. Your assignment is to work the Avalauncher, a compressed-gas-powered gun that fires explosive projectiles onto slopes too distant or dangerous for patrollers to approach on skis.

At the Avalanche HQ you assemble the charges. The explosive with a blasting cap is assembled into the mini rocket by sliding the tail fin on. It's a tight fit, and you have to work it on without banging the cap. Inside the tail fin there's a pin and a striker and just before you load the avalauncher, you pull the cotter pin out making the charge live.

Once you have assembled 20 charges, you load the snowmobile and ride up to the Avalauncher, targeting the large and popular Alpha Bowl off to the side of the main ski runs. You and your co-worker put 18 shots up into the area needing control, and nothing is moving. You have hit the cliff, hit the rolls, and pitches, and pillows, all through the area, everywhere you want. Nothings is moving.

(1). Write down your cues, goals, and what are you thinking/doing.
Do not skip ahead

Thoughts and Actions of the Expert 1

I never felt comfortable around the Avalauncher and its explosives. If you're using a safety fuse, it's got a little staple that supposed to divert 40,000 volts and when you're wearing nylon clothing, you can generate more than that on a dry windy ridge. That electricity could trigger the charge, so you handle them gently, not throwing them around. You don't want to have anything sparking.

After the 18 shots, I said, "You know what, let's just ski up there and we'll dig some holes figure out what's going on, because nothing's moving" and my co-worker said, "Yeah, I kind of feel the same way."

But then he says, "I don't want to take those charges apart" and I said "I don't either. Let's fire the shots." Neither of us wanted to take them apart or take them back because it is a bit tricky. So I said, "Yeah it's two shots, let's just fire them off".

Ski resorts are cheap. They don't want to pay for more explosives than are necessary to do the job so using the extra two charges was not an easy decision.

With the next shot up there that thing went wall to wall, side to side, right to ground. If neither of us had objected to taking these loads apart I would have skied in there and possibly into a trigger. Maybe I wouldn't have skied onto the trigger, but we would have opened it to people and maybe then the trigger never gets hit. If so, it would load with more snow and with another shoot it might come out. It's not a guarantee that people would have died but there was an instability that we knew might be there and managed to trigger.

So just about anybody doing avalanche control, if they shot 18 shots up there and hit all the spots they wanted hit and nothing went, yeah, most would've made the call that the slope is stable.

The only thing that saved our bacon was a fear; not a fear, a reluctance, to take the charges apart. Sliding around with these things in the case on the back of the sled you weren't gonna blow yourself up but there's an element of hazard there.

End of Scenario

The Expert's Reflections ...

You are looking for the triggers. You don't want to put a bunch of bombs into non trigger zones. Even when you're choosing your target, you're trying to think how that looks from the last time I was here. Maybe that looks like it's filled in, now there's a huge pillow built in there. You're looking for those kinds of things.

If you were a ski guide, and worked five years of avalanche control first, ski cutting slopes and all of that, you would have learned using all that immediate feedback information that you could then use in guiding people safely.

Guides look at the terrain trying to figure out where they're not going to hit a trigger. They don't want to skin up (or ski down) through a trigger zone and have everything release. So their whole training is based on like how can we get up this ridge or access that terrain safely? They take the safest route even if they're not in slide terrain.

Like when you make it down a slope and it doesn't slide, the slope is not necessarily safe. It might be a massive slope and maybe there's only one trigger like the one we found on Alpha Bowl, and no one's ever gonna hit it but having a better idea of where those triggers are helps your decision making.

We were always finding out what happened the day before and the day before that. All the information about snow accumulation, wind speed, wind direction, relative humidity. These are the things you thought about in the mountains. All of the information you're bringing in determines how you'll approach every situation.

If snow is disturbed and age hardened there's less chance of ski slope going - not that they don't go, they do go. So there's less chance of a skied slope sliding. To get a sense of it, you look at the slope, you look at what's happened on it, you look at the slope angle, you look at the aspect. Every day we went out as a control group looking at all of that. You're probably digging a hole every day looking at the crystals, the structure of the snow, and you're doing a weekly profile and you're putting all of that information together.

I don't think anybody ever knows 100% for sure it would be a safe spot.

Editor's Note: The Avalauncher is no longer used in Canada.

End of the Expert's Reflections

What are the five key points you developed?

Key Points Generated by ChatGPT-4

Note: OpenAI has attached the following to its webpage "ChatGPT can make mistakes. Check important info." Do you agree with what has been summarized?

Assessment of Avalanche Control Effectiveness:

After firing 18 shots into various key areas (cliffs, rolls, pitches, pillows) of a target like the Alpha Bowl and seeing no movement, it's critical to reassess the stability of the slope. Multiple impacts with no results often suggest stability, but it can be misleading.

Decision-Making Under Uncertainty:

When initial shots don't trigger avalanches, consider further investigation or additional shots before assuming the slope is safe. In this case, firing the last charge triggered a significant release, potentially averting a disaster.

Terrain and Trigger Zone Identification:

Focus on identifying trigger zones and avoiding them when possible. Accurate knowledge of terrain and recent snow conditions is crucial. Use past experiences and current observations to target potential weak spots and make informed decisions.

Comprehensive Snowpack Analysis:

Continuously gather data on snow accumulation, wind conditions, and snow structure. Regularly dig snow pits and analyze crystal structures to understand the snowpack's stability, integrating this information into your avalanche control strategy.

The idea is to embrace the uncertainty. If something doesn't make sense, don't ignore it.

"Until we know we are wrong, being wrong feels exactly like being right."

Kathryn Schultz

Stepping Off - Avalanche Control: Assessing Hidden Triggers.

Read the following scenario developed from an interview with an expert and stop at the decision point question as indicated by the statement...

"Write down your cues, goals, and what are you thinking/doing."

The following is very important and is how you will learn using this method.

Put yourself in the place of the expert and write down what you would be thinking and or doing if you were in that situation. **If you don't take the time to do this... you won't learn.**

Note that the information in the scenario might be incomplete, much the same as it would be in the real world.

<u>Do not skip ahead</u>. Reading ahead to see what the expert has done before you have put your thoughts down, will negate the value of this exercise.

After you have put your thoughts on paper refer to the next page "Thoughts of the Expert...". Have you differed or missed something? Think about that.

Continue reading the scenario sections, writing down your thoughts, and reading those of the expert until you come to the end. Reflect about the situation. In the same position, would you make the same decisions? What would be the outcome of those decisions?

Read the Expert's reflections to gain context and deeper understanding.

During your review of the expert's scenario and their thoughts, write down 5 key points. Compare your 5 to those developed by ChatGPT-4.

If you have any questions or comments, please reach out to
helicourse@gmail.com

"Show me the incentive and I will show you the outcome." Charlie Munger

Stepping Off 1

You are working avalanche control at a Rocky Mountain ski resort. It is midwinter and you have a good understanding of the snowpack. Today you are on top of the mountain with a team of two other avalanche experts, Alpha and Bravo, looking to control Zulu, one of the chutes that go down the front side. It is one of the regulars, with a steep entrance 50m wide, a rocky edge on the left, a cliff drop off on the right side, and several boulders strewn throughout. New snow has accumulated and is deemed a hazard.

During the winter you and your team have controlled the size of the cornice that is on one side of the entrance, and it is not of immediate concern. Zulu starts with that cornice on one side of it tapering into a steep roll onto the slope as you move further down the ridge.

The cornice isn't overhung very much because you are always working on these cornices, reducing their size by kicking them off or shoveling them.

You have brought hand charges with you in your backpack.

You throw a hand charge into the sweet spot of the slope, it explodes, nothing happens, the slope remains stable.

(1). Write down your cues, goals, and what are you thinking/doing.
<u>Do not skip ahead.</u>

Thoughts and Actions of the Expert 1

You start your day reviewing all knowledge and accumulated information.

Avalanche control is usually done with a team of 2 (recommend a minimum of 3 for backcountry touring with only 1 person exposed at any time) with each team is assigned a specific work zone.

The goal is to ski through the zone, assess terrain stability and hazards, then take appropriate steps to stabilize terrain and mitigate hazards. More information is needed to make the determination whether Zulu is safe to open for the public.

Common practice is to toss in a hand charge first if we feel snow has accumulated or weight of snow has increased.

A ski cut is the next option but one has to assess the slope and know the outcome of a failed ski cut. Where will you be carried to if caught in slide? What hazards will you be exposed to (terrain traps, rocks, trees, cliffs) if caught? Is it survivable?

It is important to identify all safe zones and ski quickly from safe zone to safe zone (minimize the time that you are exposed).

DON'T SKI CUT IF THE OUTCOME IS NOT SURVIVABLE.

The plan is to start high to minimize how much snow is above you, slip off the end of the cornice, ski cut it, and come out back up further down the ridge.
Even if a slide is triggered during the ski cut, the ridge must be safely attainable.

Stepping Off 2

Alpha jumps off, lands under the cornice, ski cuts the top of the slope, then pops back up on the ridge.

The slope does not react.

After Alpha ski cuts the top of Zulu, you ask, "What do you think?"

Alpha says "Jeez I don't know. There's something that just doesn't feel right in there." So, you throw another bomb with no result. Bravo says, "I'm going to go out and kind of sidestep across the slope and just poke around and feel."

Bravo works cross slope, does a kick turn and comes back and says, "I'm not sensing this is good either."

You're not getting any releases, you've tossed 2 bombs, and you've done ski cutting, you've poked around. Nothing has happened.

The ski area is on the radio wondering what's up. Your supervisor calls asking what are you doing? Can you open that yet?

(2). Write down your cues, goals, and what are you thinking/doing.

<u>Do not skip ahead.</u>

Thoughts and Actions of the Expert 2

So, then I said "Alpha, you know what? I'm going to poke around one more time." So, I went out there and I'm poking around below the cornice and just kind of in the same spot a little lower than Bravo's tracks. Under the cornice, it's hard slab and I can feel myself step off that into loose snow. Then the whole thing, the cornice, everything - gone.

As the avalanche happened I sunk into the snow and was pushed downhill and up against a boulder. The snow was flowing over me and around me. On that side of Zulu, it kind of rolls over a cliff, so if I hadn't been pushed up against that rock, I would have gone over the cliff. It was a learning experience, not to be repeated. Perhaps terrain with those characteristics should become a permanent closure area.

Afterwards I'm thinking about this. I had skied the back bowl one time, and nothing happened all the way down. It was all stable but when I got to the bottom, I could feel myself slip off the firm base of the slab. I heard that whoomphing sound and then saw fracture lines running all over.

These massive fracture lines were of a huge settlement running all through the bowl. It didn't slide, it just settled and sat there. I had hit the trigger that was at the end of this slab, below the fresh snow. Kind of like when you're skiing not bottomless powder, but you've got a base. Similarly on Zulu, it was when I got into the loose snow at the end of the slab, that the slab above me avalanched. That is where the trigger was.

After 2 or 3 similar events (control work under a cornice) we realized that we needed to keep this "end of slab/unconsolidated snow" interface in mind when doing control work. It seemed like the unconsolidated snow was not providing support for the cornice and its slab that extended down below the cornice. This slab/snow interface was a weak point and an area that needed to be tickled (ski cut or bombed) to stabilize.

Options:

- look for similar areas (cornice slab above weaker snow pack) that are low angle not liable to slide. Use these areas to poke around feeling things out.
- use a larger/faster explosive to hunt for this weakness.
- in situations without access to explosives (ski touring) consider dropping cornice onto the slope. Just need to hit the weakness with a bunch of weight. We usually carry a ruesch block cord which can be used for cutting cornice.

End of Scenario

The Expert's Reflections ...

Early morning when you're trying to open the slopes and people are waiting there, waiting for the open sign, there's a little more pressure. How quickly are you guys working, what steps are you taking, are you sure you can't get by with one bomb and one ski cut? Ski areas like to say, "We had everything open by 10:00 today" and that attracts people. That affects your decision making.

Avalanche control is answering the question "where are the triggers?"

You are looking for the triggers and to release the snow that is a threat. You don't want to put a bunch of bombs into non trigger zones. Even when you're choosing your target, you're trying to think about the last time you were there, what's different? Where are the triggers? Perhaps you might say "That section looks like it is loaded with new snow, it's a huge pillow filled in there. That is a possible trigger."

You don't want to be triggering slides and dropping cornices on slopes with people below. Controlling access and exposure at a ski area is much safer than the backcountry. You don't want random people out there just kicking something off without knowing exactly what is going to happen. At a ski hill, you know who's around, where it's going to run, what's the maximum path. In the backcountry these types of slopes should be avoided, especially in the Rockies.

Predicting a big event is difficult. You can look at the trees and the forest at the flanks of slide path and you can kind of tell the 60 year history of what was the biggest slide there. But you can't tell what a 200 year one is because a lot of the vegetation is back in and if you drop it, you might cause the biggest slide in the 200 years and have little idea of where it is going to go.

The feedback when working in avalanche control is excellent for learning how to spot triggers. Backcountry skiing rarely gives you the same feedback.

For example, when you ski down a slope and it doesn't slide, the slope is not necessarily safe. It might be a massive slope and maybe there's only one trigger and maybe no one is ever going to hit it but having a better idea of where those triggers are helps in ski route decision making.

I don't think anybody ever knows 100% for sure if the slope is safe to ski cut, so the plan would be to ski from safe spot to safe spot. You don't want to go across on a slowly when ski cutting, you're going across the slope really fast. You might have to change the angle you cut the slope at depending on the depth of the snow. You have to look for a safe spot far enough down that you can have a steeper angle.

Sometimes we just go across almost stomping it. You're just skiing slowly across trying to create more force down to a second weak layer that is buried a little deeper but you're not as worried about it pulling out the same way because it's not as reactive.

All the information you're bringing in determines how you'll approach every situation.

End of the Expert's Reflections

What are the five key points you developed?

Key Points Generated by ChatGPT-4

Note: OpenAI has attached the following to its webpage "ChatGPT can make mistakes. Check important info." Do you agree with what has been summarized?

Thorough Preparation and Information Review:

Start each day by reviewing all available data on the snowpack, weather, and previous control efforts. Ensure your team of at least three experts is fully briefed on the day's plan and potential hazards specific to the chute you're working on, such as Zulu.

Controlled Assessment and Methodical Approach:

Begin by throwing a hand charge into the suspect area. If no reaction occurs, proceed with a ski cut, ensuring to understand and mitigate the risks involved.

Identify safe zones and move quickly from one to another to minimize exposure. Avoid ski cutting if the outcome is not survivable due to terrain traps or other hazards.

Team Communication and Decision-Making:

Maintain constant communication with your team members (Alpha and Bravo) to share observations and gut feelings about the stability of the slope. If initial measures (bombs and ski cuts) do not trigger an avalanche, deliberate with your team about the next steps, considering further probing or different explosive strategies.

Understanding Trigger Points and Terrain Characteristics:

Pay special attention to the interface between hard slabs and unconsolidated snow, especially under cornices, as these are critical trigger points. Use larger or faster explosives to hunt for these weak points, or consider dropping cornices onto the slope to induce a release.

Safety and Public Communication:

Keep the ski area informed of your progress and any delays. The pressure to open slopes quickly should not compromise safety.

Control access to the slopes rigorously to prevent unauthorized individuals from triggering avalanches. Ensure that all control work is completed before allowing public access to potentially hazardous areas.

Count to Five - choosing terrain for a group

Read the following scenario developed from an interview with an expert and stop at the decision point question as indicated by the statement...

"Write down your cues, goals, and what are you thinking/doing."

The following is very important and is how you will learn using this method.

Put yourself in the place of the expert and write down what you would be thinking and or doing if you were in that situation. **If you don't take the time to do this... you won't learn.**

Note that the information in the scenario might be incomplete, much the same as it would be in the real world.

<u>Do not skip ahead</u>. Reading ahead to see what the expert has done before you have put your thoughts down, will negate the value of this exercise.

After you have put your thoughts on paper refer to the next page "Thoughts of the Expert...". Have you differed or missed something? Think about that.

Continue reading the scenario sections, writing down your thoughts, and reading those of the expert until you come to the end. Reflect about the situation. In the same position, would you make the same decisions? What would be the outcome of those decisions?

Read the Expert's reflections to gain context and deeper understanding.

During your review of the expert's scenario and their thoughts, write down 5 key points. Compare your 5 to those developed by ChatGPT-4.

If you have any questions or comments, please reach out to
helicourse@gmail.com

The most important story is the one you tell yourself.

Count to Five 1

You are in the Coast Mountains guiding a heliski group of five clients sharing a Bell 407 with another two groups skiing in the same area. The snowpack disparities are consistent throughout the zone. The hazard rating is considerable (3 out of 5), with a layer of facets on a crust buried 50 cm down creating a persistent slab problem.

There is no evidence of recent natural activity. Nobody is triggering anything on this beautiful day. You aren't ski cutting anything. You have been skiing a fair amount of manageable, supported, open terrain without so much as a whoomph, cracking, or any natural activity observed.

There is good flow today, the groups are moving well, and now it's time for the last run. Because of logistics, timing, and snow quality you choose to ski the same run again.

On the flight up, you landmark the route you would like to ski. This takes you a short distance away from where you were previously skiing, but still offers a relatively safe route down to the final pitch, which is a moraine feature. The moraine is northwest facing 5500 feet above sea level and partly a cross-loaded slope. You have been skiing the moraine from skier's right (or east), where the terrain is more supported, to skier's left (or west), where the terrain steepens and is more convoluted, generally avoiding these more committing skier's left parcels of terrain.

You have traditionally skied the standard safe line of the run and moraine but not necessarily the moraine line you are now considering. The moraine portion tends to be a little bit more sheltered and usually offers a good, final pitch of skiing before you reach the helicopter pickup at the bottom.

When you arrive at the top of the moraine, the ground picture has changed. It is a little more challenging, steeper, more convoluted in appearance, and less supported than you have thought from the air.

1. Write down your cues, goals, and what you are thinking/doing.

<u>Do not skip ahead.</u>

Thoughts and Actions of the Expert 1

I had already skied farther over to the skier's right (east) on the moraine previously and so had my colleagues. The terrain there was more supported. Given the lack of reactivity in the snowpack this day and despite being aware of the avalanche problem, I regarded this skier's left line on the moraine on the flight up and thought "I believe I can make the line work with some good group control".

However, once I arrived at the entry to the line that I was considering, something just didn't feel right. I somewhat quickly concluded that perhaps I was attempting to 'thread the needle' on a day where we needed to keep wider margins. One thing we know about persistent slab problems is to avoid trying to 'outthink' them.

The ground picture had changed from what I thought I had observed from the air. Terrain assessments and landmarking effectively can sometimes be challenging when you're climbing quickly in a helicopter. What I had noted was:

1. the line I was considering was accessible, and
2. it was inviting for all the reasons I mentioned before, and
3. I knew I had an 'out' before committing myself to the crux. So, it was worth going down to have a look but when I arrived, the ground picture changed.

After arriving at the crux, something intuitive prompted me to think that this isn't the right time to ski this line. Last run of the day, when accidents tend to happen, still relatively deep in the range and far away from base were some of the rational reasons that came to mind for not continuing with my original plan. Why take on the risk?

And so, my decision was that this is a little bit too big of a meatball to chew, especially at this time of day.

Prior to considering these factors, I had regrouped my clients just behind the apex of the moraine in a safe location. After making the decision to not ski the line, my instructions to the clients were to avoid the slope immediately below our position (the line in question) and follow my traverse back to the skier's right to the more supported terrain that was skied previously. I was quite specific that they should stay precisely in my traverse line or just above it while moving back toward the east. The group acknowledged these instructions and seemingly understood the objective.

Definitely avoid the worst outcome while trying for the best." Rory Sutherland

Count to Five 2

So, you establish the traverse line out to the skier's right and you have asked the clients to begin the traverse with some spacing, once they start to see you ski. You traverse right and then start skiing down. The first client follows, the second client follows, and then the third client follows but does so below the traverse line you've set. It is at this point that a healthy skier accidental size 2 is initiated. A client shouts "Avalanche!" The crown of the avalanche varies between 20 cm to 80 cm thick, a 75 m wide, and runs approximately 100 m.

(2). Write down your cues, goals, and what you are thinking/doing.
<u>Do not skip ahead.</u>

Thoughts and Actions of the Expert 2

When you are guiding, you always want to leave yourself an out. I knew that if something was going to happen, I would maneuver hard right to the increasingly more supported terrain that had no exposure to overhead hazard. When I heard my client yell 'Avalanche!', I veered hard right, stopped, then turned toward the scene unfolding behind me.

Count to Five 3

You look back and your first client arrives without problem. The second client also arrives while the third client (the person that triggered this avalanche), was able to maneuver far skier's right before eventually regrouping with you. The fourth client has started a slow traverse toward you, but you do not know where your fifth client is.

(3). Write down your cues, goals, and what you are thinking/doing.

<u>Do not skip ahead.</u>

Thoughts and Actions of the Expert 3

An avalanche response begins with assessing how many, if any, clients are missing. This is important information to pass along to your dispatch and may influence the level of response that is initiated. I was only able to account for four of my clients, so I began my count again with the hope that I had miscounted and there were actually five souls present and not four.

All of this happens within seconds. I began reaching for the PTT (push to talk button) on my radio to alert my immediate colleagues and have them undertake an aerial survey of the scene. I was also preparing to make a second radio call afterward to our dispatch and initiate our emergency response plan for a 'Code A' (or avalanche response) when I noticed something moving at the top of the moraine.

There is a single western white bark pine tree that grows at the top of this moraine just behind the apex. From my position, it appeared as though a branch was moving. I soon realized that this moving branch was my fifth client, side stepping up to the regroup position from behind the apex of the moraine and was never in any danger. Interestingly, this client was unaware that the slope had released. I stood down any call for a rescue response but did ask one of my colleagues to access the crown and perform a fracture line profile so we could have some information and data about the release for our afternoon guide meeting and debrief. After regrouping my clients, we proceeded to the pickup location and headed home.

I'm not sure if it crossed my mind to attempt a call on the guest radio to my fifth client re: his status because my colleagues were already airborne and were in the better position to assist.

The line that I skied to the regroup location on top of the moraine hadn't been tracked up, so that was part of the appeal. Fresh snow without tracks on the final run. It would have been safer to ski nearer to our old tracks and stay away from the section of steepening unsupported moraine.

My other colleague at that point had landed on the run and skied down to perform a fracture line profile. We confirmed that the failure layer were the facets and the bed surface was that of the crust that we were aware of.

If I had triggered the avalanche on my traverse out to the skiers right, it would have involved me, but to no great extent as that skier's right side of the avalanche lensed out and was more manageable and of less consequence.

I never really blame the clients for things that happen. I own that. I own the decision process and the communication piece. Obviously, I wasn't clear enough on where to ski and what the issue was, so that's on me.

Lesson learned for me was that when a persistent slab problem exists, that this particular run is one to leave alone to cure a while longer. It is also a run that has a history of near misses of this nature.

End of Scenario

The Expert's Reflections ...

The goals for the day were of course to get everyone back safely. That is always the overarching goal every day. That's not negotiable.

It's a heart dropping moment when you realize that you may have killed a client. You have that sinking feeling for a split second and then you default to your training and get to work on rescuing. There is plenty of time afterward to deal with your emotions.

Since then, I've further realized not to negotiate with my little voice. One of the best lessons I've learned in my career is not to explain away the hazard. This is key. Sometimes all you can attribute your decision to is a feeling. Respect this about yourself.

It's possible that if a novice guide had found themselves in that position, they may have entered further into the terrain before something happened one way or the other.

It's important to maintain margins as guides. We train our clients in rescue procedures, but we don't know how competent they will be in the event of an actual rescue. And since it may be you under the snow, your wider margins become a kind of insurance for yourself.

Sometimes you are constrained by logistics and timing, helicopter fuel cycle requirements, snow quality, and terrain options. In this instance, it just made sense to stay where we were. We had a great run previously in that same general terrain and it was an easy one to repeat. I think in terms of the decision process some of the drive may have been the scarcity heuristics (when an object is thought to be scarce, it is considered more valuable).

Generally, you're looking to give the clients a good, final run. It's been a great day, the group is skiing well, there's been plenty of good skiing, and you'd like to end on a solid note.

Having radios in the group has just been a game changer. One of the best things that a client can do during a rescue is to remember to make the radio call. Clients should be concise, clear, and make contact with the group's guide, another guide, or the pilot. These other professionals will initiate the emergency response plan.

I think it's quite common in the avalanche patch for professional practitioners to share the attitude of invulnerability. It can't happen to me. This is what I do. I do it well and I can manage it. You feel that you can guide groups in the worst of mountain conditions and make the day work. And generally you can, but this isn't always the case. I think we need to realize that, indeed, it can happen to me.

We are in the business of balancing the commercial imperative with safety. Be aware of your own hazardous attitudes and make good decisions. At the end of the day, it's just skiing. None of it though, is worth hurting people for.

Snow profiles are point observations. Spatial variability is a factor and snow profiles are only one, small piece of the puzzle. There's almost always instability in the mountains. Where you choose to dig and investigate is important. Maybe it's a wind loaded area with just two metres of decomposing fragments and rounded grains. But if you descend into the terrain where the snowpack has changed but you base your decisions on what you observed higher up, then you could get yourself into trouble.

So, we're always trying to reduce our uncertainty by knowing as much as we can about the snow on any given day. This means lots of investigation. If I can offer you a bit of advice, it's to be curious. Poke into the snow a lot. You don't need to dig snow profiles everywhere, but you can get your gloved hand in the snow and quickly know the character of the snow. You can push a ski pole into the top meter and get a quick sense of whether there is firmer snow sitting above a layer of soft snow which may constitute a slab problem. These simple tests take almost no time, and you can perform many of them. Doing so allows you to update your baseline about the snow in an ongoing way, which may help to reduce uncertainty and allow you to make more effective decisions.

Try to always leave yourself an out when you're moving through the mountains. We try to default to terrain choices. Snowpack is the problem; terrain is the solution.

I'm finding one of the key things to developing the intuitive sense is closing the loop. I might be just pointing out the obvious, but getting feedback, even as a senior guide, is so important.

An after-action review or hotwash or a debrief provides that framework. It's not about who did what, but what happened, what occurred, what was your greatest risk that day, and how did you manage it? These discussions are just gold mines and full of important information.

Start a good habit by processing your day in that same way, debrief yourself. When you ask yourself for an answer, you are going to be honest. The only way you might miss good feedback is if you're just genuinely ignorant, in which case the feedback you need would be provided by a knowledgeable colleague. Debrief with yourself, friends, and colleagues. "If I were to go out and repeat the same circuit I did today for tomorrow, would I change anything?"

I think some of us can be better with the communication piece, not assuming that other people are aware of the same thing. If it's on your mind, it's worth mentioning. We can have a concern or maybe think it is a little bit sporty for today's conditions. We should not just assume that the other guides will reach that same conclusion themselves. I would say don't be shy, be vulnerable.

Find a good mentor. Mentorship is so key in this business.

End of the Expert's Reflections

What are the five key points you developed?

Key Points Generated by ChatGPT-4

Note: OpenAI has attached the following to its webpage "ChatGPT can make mistakes. Check important info." Do you agree with what has been summarized?

Terrain and Snowpack Assessment:

Consistently evaluate terrain and snowpack conditions. Persistent slab problems require heightened caution. Trust your instincts if something feels off, as conditions on the ground may differ from aerial assessments.

Regularly perform simple snowpack tests (e.g., hand probing, ski pole tests) to understand snow layers and potential weaknesses, especially when navigating complex or steep terrain.

Effective Group Control and Communication:

Keep clients informed about safe routes and stress the importance of following your precise instructions. Ensure everyone understands the risks and safety protocols.

Use radios effectively to maintain communication with your team and clients, especially during critical moments or emergencies.

Decision-Making and Safety Margins:

Avoid taking unnecessary risks, especially late in the day or when far from base. Stick to known safe lines and resist the urge to push boundaries, particularly when dealing with persistent slab problems. Always leave yourself and your group an "out" in case conditions change unexpectedly.

Emergency Preparedness and Response:

Be prepared to quickly assess and respond to an avalanche incident. Know how to account for all clients and initiate a rescue plan if necessary.

Train clients in rescue procedures and ensure they know how to make concise radio calls in case of an emergency. Clear communication can significantly aid in coordinating a swift response.

Continuous Learning and Feedback:

Conduct debriefs after each day to analyze decisions, assess risks, and gather feedback. This helps in understanding what worked well and what could be improved.

Seek mentorship and engage in ongoing learning. Sharing experiences with more experienced guides can provide invaluable insights and help develop your intuitive sense for recognizing hazards.

The Gray Zone - Alphas that need direction

Read the following scenario developed from an interview with an expert and stop at the decision point question as indicated by the statement...

"Write down your cues, goals, and what are you thinking/doing."

The following is very important and is how you will learn using this method.

Put yourself in the place of the expert and write down what you would be thinking and or doing if you were in that situation. **If you don't take the time to do this... you won't learn.**

Note that the information in the scenario might be incomplete, much the same as it would be in the real world.

<u>Do not skip ahead</u>. Reading ahead to see what the expert has done before you have put your thoughts down, will negate the value of this exercise.

After you have put your thoughts on paper refer to the next page "Thoughts of the Expert...". Have you differed or missed something? Think about that.

Continue reading the scenario sections, writing down your thoughts, and reading those of the expert until you come to the end. Reflect about the situation. In the same position, would you make the same decisions? What would be the outcome of those decisions?

Read the Expert's reflections to gain context and deeper understanding.

During your review of the expert's scenario and their thoughts, write down 5 key points. Compare your 5 to those developed by ChatGPT-4.

If you have any questions or comments, please reach out to
helicourse@gmail.com

The most fun skiing is exactly where avalanches happen.

The Gray Zone 1

You have just begun working as the guide at a back country ski lodge that has few bookings. The only other staff is your partner, who is the chef. To fill up the place, it has been rented out to a group of ten self-catered, self-guided skiers who have just arrived. The understanding is that they need neither the chef nor you, the guide. They have skied here previously and plan to spend the next five days skiing the entire tenure. You know some of them well and others only as acquaintances. The group as a whole you recognize as generally having a weak backcountry skiing skill set. You want to give them the best experience and hope they will be satisfied.

(1). Write down your cues, goals, and what you are thinking/doing.

<u>Do not skip ahead.</u>

Thoughts and Actions of the Expert 1

I had suggested some parameters about stability, the unstable layer in the snowpack, things to avoid, and things to be a bit aware of. I put that out at the beginning of the trip to the group. We did a little bit of avalanche transceiver training but other than that they were off, choosing their own objectives. I was uncomfortable with the "self-guided and see you at the lodge for supper" program having only led structured programs in the past.

The Gray Zone 2

It is day one of skiing and you have chosen to ski with your partner and follow the group. They all tag along behind the Alpha Dog leader, who has experience but no training. The ten skiers head up into the alpine to the top of the North Face Chute.

There is quite a bit of new snow with good traveling conditions, so they can get into a lot of places fairly easily. The two and half meter interior snowpack has 50 to 60 centimeters of new snow sitting on a layer of surface hoar. Underneath is a settled snowpack, the crystals rounded and well consolidated but there is that unstable layer that is of concern. They do not dig a pit or seem to gather any relevant information enroute.

You know the North Face Chute is avalanche terrain and is a big consequence run if anything slides.

The Alpha Dog has the option to ski down close to the up track on the more moderate terrain. Instead, you watch from a hundred metres back as he decides to drop into the North Face Chute, a north facing bowl that is a very exposed, wind loaded area.

(2). Write down your cues, goals, and what you are thinking/doing.

<u>Do not skip ahead.</u>

Thoughts and Actions of the Expert 2

I would never have done that. I would not have dropped in without understanding the snowpack. I would have tickled the edge of the chute or found out more about that particular area, but he just dropped in, and people started following him. That was really uncomfortable for me because I knew these people. I was trying to let them go and have their time. My partner and I just stayed at the top. We didn't follow them because I had made my decision not to go in there.

To my relief, they didn't release anything.

The group skied down into this north facing basin and then had to climb back up the way they had gone in. So, they were entering it from the top and then they were climbing up into what I still considered to be an issue in the snowpack. There was a layer that I was concerned with so that's why I didn't want to go into places like that, alpine wind loaded slopes.

It worked out OK that day. When they got out, I think I said something about my concern of them skiing dangerous slopes. But they were self-guided, and I was trying to figure this out. I had to let them go as much as I was able.

The Gray Zone 3

You have a nice evening in the lodge and then it is back out the next day to another run called Zulu. You shadow them as they follow this one fellow, the Alpha Dog. He knows terrain, so he is able to get up into some areas of good skiing, the same places you would go. So that's cool, that is all fine and you are following them right up into the alpine. It is pretty mellow terrain. But when you get to the subalpine and alpine interface you clue into the fact that he is planning to ski an area of steep chutes, not quite couloirs, right at tree line with good wind effect and wind loading.

You are very concerned now that, even though you are not guiding this group, they will get into trouble because they can't seem to understand the hazard of the hidden layer. You need to get the point across how dangerous their decision making, and route choices are. The conversation last night was "We know we are safe because we got back at the end of the day".

(3). Write down your cues, goals, and what you are thinking/doing.

<u>Do not skip ahead.</u>

Thoughts and Actions of the Expert 3

There is one chute in particular that I was really concerned about, and they were going to drop right into it. So, what was in my head was "I need to show these guys what's going on. I need to demonstrate it, because even though I could dig a pit and show them the layers, it's not the same. With these people it won't register". So anyway, I was with this group, and they were about to drop into this zone where this one chute was and I said, "Hang on. I'm going to ski cut this before you guys go in."

So, I did. I had a plan. The entrance was maybe 25 meters wide. There was a very prominent break when you dropped into this thing; the slope angle changed to 40°. So, I hit it really hard and fast at that transition. There was a small group of mature timber on the other side of this chute. I remember going "OK, well if something gets weird I'll hopefully hold my momentum, get over there and grab something". As I ski cut it, I had a lot of momentum. I remember that I was hitting it hard, stomping on it as I was trained to do.

I wasn't really expecting what happened. It released catastrophically, maybe 10 meters above me, not at my skis as I was hoping. I'm pretty familiar with cutting avalanches with my skis but this broke above me, quite a ways above me, with a metre crown, so a huge amount of snow. It was moving on surface hoar and that was the issue. It moved very fast.

Once it fractured, I thought "OK, this is released". I had momentum and I remember just smashing into this big tree and grabbing it. I was on the downhill side but there was so much mass that (my partner who stayed on top, watching, will remember this) it just went right over me and it took one of my poles. Anyways, I was able to hang onto this tree and the debris went over me and went into the run out.

After everything settled down and I was able to stand up and say "I'm still here" to the people waiting safely above the crown. All was fine. The only way I had to ski down was on the bed surface. Everybody else could go around and obviously I didn't have to say, "Don't come down here".

Choosing that slope instead of a smaller one was an error. I actually compromised myself and my better judgement by trying to prove a point. The consequences were too big. It was a poor choice, that's why it's a strong memory. I could have really got hurt.

End of Scenario

The Expert's Reflections ...

I was going to show those guys that they didn't know what I knew. "I'll show them" I thought, and I crossed a line. I should not have cut that slope. I should have cut the one that was two chutes over which had far less consequences but I didn't because I was pissed off and stressed out.

You think about the avalanche triangle of terrain, hazard, and consequence. What conditions do we have here? You need all three. Is the slope steep enough to slide, do we have an instability, and then what are the consequences? That's the big one, and on Zulu the consequences were huge. Well, that being the case, what's your option? Do you have an option to go around? And that's the hard one right there, to say no because of all that ego and commercial momentum. You've got these people who have come from all over and paid a ton of money.

One time I had very strong skiers from France. They were doing a lot of filming and they wanted to do bigger things that I wasn't willing to let them do like jumping into features. They were saying "Let us go do that, why are we just getting this mellow stuff?" I found was I was getting pushed. I wanted to give them the best experience, so they'd be satisfied. They'd be pleased, maybe I had thoughts even as naive or immature as "Oh they'll like me and give me a bigger tip" or something as immature as that. That is real. You want them to like you, want them to have a good time, and forgetting that holy ****, there's a layer down there that I'm not really sure about.

The motivation to get people into the best terrain that is appropriate for that day is the Gray Zone; good skiing, safe skiing, pushing the envelope of safety to please the guests. That's very tricky because we can't do a test pit or shear test on every slope you're skiing, so you're making these very quick decisions based on extrapolation of information from the indexes that you've created from other areas appropriate to that slope, at that elevation, slope incline, aspect, and time of day. A change in any one of those affects the slope. It's pretty dynamic.

Do you have a sense of where to find those sweet spots, the avalanche triggers?

Not always. I mean the mountains can look pretty uniform. What would change and create a trigger is maybe the slope angle that changed by a few degrees or the aspect has changed slightly, maybe a little more wind loading.

The whole winter you're looking at snow. Even from the valley. Early on I was taught this. All winter you watch the weather to give you a deeper understanding of the snowpack, the hazard, and the skiing conditions.

To kind of summarize and reflect on my career, the biggest one for me is to realize, in hindsight especially, I could have really messed up. At one point in my career, I thought I need to back off or I'm going to kill somebody. But you don't know that you need to back off until something happens, or you don't know till you reflect "Wow that's what it's like to ride in avalanche". I could have really done some stupid things. I was either very fortunate or I made the decision to pull back and look at it, maybe take another more moderate line then come back and step into it on the next pass and see how it goes.

The other part is that you don't know the parts that you don't know. The unknown. Well, we didn't jump in there, would it have been OK? Or would it have released? Because you avoided it, it's hard to say. Was I being overly cautious?

You are re-evaluating constantly. I do remember teaching was one of the best things for my learning. You go over this stuff again, and again, and again, and again, and again, looking at pits, like lot of pits. You get a deep understanding of the layers in the snowpack. You will think, "Oh look at that, it has changed from the previous readings".

This is important because the layers can be so different in similar areas. When it comes to differing results in the test pit, it could be just different people using a different force or maybe they're levering the column rather than shearing it, or they made the column smaller, or it was tapered, or wasn't cut accurately. The end result is that your information is subjective. Those numbers are an indication. It is only telling you about that column of snow on this aspect, at this elevation, on this mountain side, at this time of day. I hang on to that one.

When you have very limited options you're having to be more of an entertainer, and you've got to create tours. Remember it is still just skiing. Once we had such bad conditions, it was ice glazed over so if someone fell, they were going to slide for 400 meters and then there's rocks or trees or whatever it would be as the consequence. You couldn't fall, you just couldn't fall. So, you took them to areas where we were just doing touring on the gentle descents. That day it was bitterly cold. It was horrible, -30 with ice fog. It was just the hardest, the hardest work I've ever done.

I used to say to my guests "If I'm doing anything that looks stupid or that you would question, I want to hear about it" because I'm human. I didn't get into too many specifics with them but if I can't explain my decision-making process, then maybe we're not in a good place. Sometimes I'm missing something, and they will see that.

You said as a young hot head you focused on skiing the best slopes and being in charge. Did who you were and why you were out there change overtime?

Oh Yeah, especially seeing and putting a body in a bag (not my guests). That really changed things a lot. Or when you're out there with a guest and everything you touch fails, it's like, well how do you create a good experience still, you still have to be out there. Have you ever seen snow move? Trees get ripped up? Oh, that's a lot of power. There is a kind of humility in death but until you see it and the consequences, it's all abstract. The visceral experience is a strong change agent.

The primary thing you think about is that you want to bring yourself and your people home at the end of the day. When you first hear that, it doesn't make any sense because of course you're going to come home, but it does after you have been around a bit. Perhaps you ski a hazardous slope, and it fails or someone twisted ankle at 3:00 in the afternoon in January, and you've got 45 minutes of daylight, and you're still an hour and a half away from home. Now you're in the dark or you have what you're the only one with the headlight whatever. Those are things that could go wrong and maybe someone doesn't get to go home, ever.

I think if I was trying to impart anything to a young aspiring guide or technician I would say be aware of your where your head is at when you're making decisions, what is the place that your critical thinking is coming from? Are you upset because your partner had an argument in the morning or is your body aching? Maybe you're just tired of being out with these people again. Whatever the factors, is your head in a really clear place? Are you making decisions from a professional point of view or from an emotional point of view?

Ask the questions, be cautious and ask the questions so at least you have the information. When it goes wrong it's really bad and then you could just finish your career in one scenario.

Editorial Note: The scenario brings up an interesting legal question, that is the issue of a non-guided party and the responsibilities of the guide to these guests. A tough conundrum. Obviously a thorough discussion of conditions and the surface hoar layer and its distribution when the guests arrived would be in order.

End of the Expert's Reflections

What are the five key points you developed?

Key Points Generated by ChatGPT-4

Note: OpenAI has attached the following to its webpage "ChatGPT can make mistakes. Check important info." Do you agree with what has been summarized?

Initial Briefing and Training:

Conduct a thorough briefing about snow stability, potential hazards, and specific unstable layers in the snowpack. Ensure all group members understand the importance of gathering relevant information enroute and conducting stability tests.

Perform practical avalanche transceiver training with the group to ensure everyone is proficient in its use.

Assessing Group Dynamics and Leadership:

Recognize the skill levels and dynamics within the group. Even if a group has experience, assess their understanding of avalanche hazards and their decision-making process.

Monitor the "Alpha Dog" leader and intervene if their decisions put the group at risk. Emphasize the importance of informed and cautious decision-making in avalanche terrain.

Terrain and Snowpack Assessment:

Continuously evaluate the terrain and snow conditions. Understand the critical layers within the snowpack, especially any recent unstable layers like surface hoar covered by new snow.

Be cautious of wind-loaded slopes and areas with significant consequences if a slide occurs. Avoid high-risk areas unless thorough stability tests have been conducted.

Demonstrating Safe Practices:

If necessary, demonstrate safe practices such as ski cutting to assess slope stability. However, choose less consequential slopes for demonstrations to avoid high risks.

Clearly communicate the reasons behind your safety decisions to the group. Emphasize the importance of avoiding hazardous slopes despite previous successful descents.

Reflecting on Decisions and Prioritizing Safety:

Continuously re-evaluate your decisions and ensure they are based on objective assessments rather than emotional responses or external pressures.

Prioritize the safety of the group above all else. Acknowledge the importance of bringing everyone home safely at the end of the day and be prepared to make conservative decisions to ensure this outcome.

"Good judgment is usually the result of experience, and experience frequently the result of bad judgment". Robert Lovett

Bummer Dude – summer limited options and hazards

Read the following scenario developed from an interview with an expert and stop at the decision point question as indicated by the statement...

"Write down your cues, goals, and what are you thinking/doing."

The following is very important and is how you will learn using this method.

Put yourself in the place of the expert and write down what you would be thinking and or doing if you were in that situation. **If you don't take the time to do this... you won't learn.**

Note that the information in the scenario might be incomplete, much the same as it would be in the real world.

<u>Do not skip ahead</u>. Reading ahead to see what the expert has done before you have put your thoughts down, will negate the value of this exercise.

After you have put your thoughts on paper refer to the next page "Thoughts of the Expert...". Have you differed or missed something? Think about that.

Continue reading the scenario sections, writing down your thoughts, and reading those of the expert until you come to the end. Reflect about the situation. In the same position, would you make the same decisions? What would be the outcome of those decisions?

Read the Expert's reflections to gain context and deeper understanding.

During your review of the expert's scenario and their thoughts, write down 5 key points. Compare your 5 to those developed by ChatGPT-4.

If you have any questions or comments, please reach out to
helicourse@gmail.com

Bummer Dude 1

It is mid-July, and it is a brilliant blue day as featured in the advertisements. You are at a group camp and have ended up leading a group of relatively inexperienced mountaineers on an ascent of a peak in the Rockies. The five are unknown to you but they tell you that they have the skills to get up the mountain.

You have not climbed this peak before but have assessed the route from the map and because of the length of the climb, you don't have a particularly early start. Everyone is geared up for mountaineering with helmets, crampons, and ice axes. You lead the two ropes of three up the ridge and find that they talk rather more than they deliver when it comes to expertise and fitness. They are slow and you aren't confident in their footing.

You are only 2/3 of the way up the mountain when you stop before noon for a break. The terrain is getting steeper and some members of the group are visibly tired, so it's obvious to you they won't make it to the top. You explain that we cannot meet our objective and will have to return to camp. With the amount of loose rock on the way up, their poor foot placement skills, and possible rock fall, you decide that another way down is the best option.

There is a snow basin off to the right that obviously leads down towards the camp area. It takes you 20 minutes to get the people over to it and you stand on the edge assessing the terrain. The basin is 100 metres across and about 200 metres vertical. The long slope drains into a creek. Topped by some steep cliffs on "lookers left", the snow terrain on "lookers right" is just coming out of the shade and is about 45 degrees. The far side of the snow basin is beside a rocky ridge that does not look stable, but the snow slope below it looks to be in the 25 degree angle range.

(1). Write down your cues, goals, and what are you thinking/doing.

<u>Do not skip ahead.</u>

Thoughts and Actions of the Expert 1

Looking across I could see on the other side of the snow basin a fairly jagged rock ridge that did not look stable. I figured that it would be relatively easy to walk across the top of the basin below the steep cliff "lookers left" then descend on the snow beside the base of the jagged ridge. The near side of the snow basin (lookers right) was a very steep snow slope which really concerned me as it may would need crampons and belaying might be a problem.

So, I said, "Hey, here's what we're going to do. I don't want all 6 of us on the slope at the same time. So, let's short rope across the top of the snow basin below the cliff on our left then over to the far side. We will do it one rope at a time."

Testing the snow conditions, I found it was very firm, almost icy on the shady side where we were, while the sun had made the middle and far side look soft. We all put on our crampons at this time. I decided to plunge step down the softer snow on the far-left hand margin of the basin close to the edge of the jagged ridge because of the possible wet snow avalanche danger in the middle. I asked, "Does everybody understand what plunge stepping is?" They said yes, as they had traveled on snow before.

"OK," I said, "I will take one rope over and down to check it out. Don't start following me until we get off the slope to the side at the bottom." My intent was to get to a place where they could last see me where I would wave my ice axe and then they could follow.

Bummer Dude 2

You cross the basin with your rope of three to the left-hand margin of the basin and descend just beside the jagged rock ridge. You are maybe 3 or 4 metres apart, plunge stepping down in the snow with mid-calf penetration. It is wet snow, but it isn't bottomless. The two people behind are comfortable, following in my footsteps, and the other three people are still on the top, watching us descend.

You are only a couple meters out from the jagged rock ridge and the plunge stepping is good, with very quick progress. When you get down to the place where you are last able to see the party of three, you wave your ice axe on the understanding that they will wait 5 minutes then start across the top of the slope and follow your plunge step tracks down.

(2). Write down your cues, goals, and what are you thinking/doing.

<u>Do not skip ahead.</u>

Thoughts and Actions of the Expert 2

I had assumed the three were going to do what I told them and follow my tracks.

I should have mentioned the possibility of an avalanche but neglected to do so to them and assumed incorrectly they would have sensed that possibility.

My decision to put on crampons at the start was useful for the first 50 metres or so, and then the snow was soft enough for easy foot penetration.

The slope that was dangerously steep and icy on the original "lookers left side" we now looked up at that slope, and I was convinced I had made the correct decision to avoid using it while the middle of the basin looked too wet and avalanche prone.

The middle of a snow basin can be dangerous as that is where the water probably drains and there have been fatalities for some who have broken through the snow-covered creek and drowned as they went underneath the snowpack, acting as a dam, and drowned.

Plunge stepping down the left side near the edge proved to be the safest and quickest way down rather than stumbling down the rocky ridge or attempting the middle and steeper snowy parts of the basin.

One must use caution using crampons on wet snow as it can ball-up and throw one off balance and one can fall downslope. If the snow balls-up, then the ice axe should be used to hit the boot side and clear the problem.

Bummer Dude 3

You get down to the very bottom of the basin which ends up in the creek and climb off the snow below a big rock buttress. You look up and see the party of three have already crossed the top of the basin and are standing at the top of the plunge steps. You give them a wave of your ice axe. You can see they are having a conversation amongst themselves, but of course you can't hear because of the distance, and you are beside the creek.

Instead of coming down the plunge steps route, they decide to take about 6 steps off to their right towards the middle of the basin and glissade. The first one comes down and still roped to the other two, decides to start bum sliding and ends up pulling the other two off their feet. The impact of the three on the wet summer snow triggers an avalanche four metres wide that takes them downslope towards us.

They don't pull out the whole slope, just a narrow slot section of the basin. They have their ice axes out and are trying to self-arrest, but the moving mass of snow is too deep for that to work. They pass you, 10 meters away, and the whole mass of snow goes into the open creek. All you can see now in the stopped debris is one head and a couple of chunks of rope. Everything else has disappeared and the three are buried in the wet snow.

(3). Write down your cues, goals, and what are you thinking/doing.

<u>Do not skip ahead.</u>

Thoughts and Actions of the Expert 3

I was waiting on the rock buttress at the bottom of the basin to protect us from the possibility of an avalanche.

To my dismay, although I was shouting at them and the other two members of my group were pointing towards the plunge steps, they decided they were going to glissade. Of course, we just watched with bated breath knowing of the potential avalanche danger.

The first one down decided to bum slide while roped to the other two. I mean, you have no control over this situation.

In retrospect, where did I make the mistake?

I didn't realize they were going to ignore my instructions. I should have gone halfway down and stopped where I could still see them and then make sure they were doing OK. They could have stopped on the rocks beside me, and we could have continued our descent. I think that would have been a better way for the other party follow to a meeting point rather than my trusting in the fact that they were going to come down in my steps. I would have been able to yell at them from there not to glissade.

As we watched the avalanche that they started, there was nothing we could do. There was nothing they could do. It was a terrible feeling for all of us.

I was worried about the sides of the basin pulling in and creating a larger avalanche. When you have a curved basin if the centre goes, the sides can collapse.

In wet snow your survival time is measured not in minutes, but literally in seconds. I was afraid of them suffocating. We stayed roped together and ran over to the one person's head that was clear of the snow then grabbed chunks of rope to try to find the other two. Because their long coils of rope had undone and ours was there as well, there was rope everywhere and we just didn't know where the other two people were. So, we kept pulling sections of rope until we located them. We dug them out with our hands and got their faces exposed.

They were conscious. They were very, very wet, and very, very scared. We saw a fair amount of blood around. We had to completely dig them out one by one, to find that this one fellow's ice axe had really raked his arm. The crampons and the rocks in the creek had also added to injuries. We had to dry out the injured and bleeding areas before using dressings to stop the bleeds.

This whole process to get them out and retrieve all the equipment probably took us close to 30 minutes. Now we had three hypothermic, injured and not particularly fit people and we had to make the descent down into the valley back to camp. We had them put on their extra warm clothes, plus stuff out of our packs because we still had a lot of travel to accomplish.

The creek flowed down a steep face that we could not safely rappel down, so we had to climb up a distance and traverse out of the gully then down a very steep forested mountain slope.

They were badly banged up in terms of their joints and contusions and they were **in** shock. We literally couldn't descend for more than about 10-15 minutes before they had to sit down and rest. So, I had two fit people and three injured people. As a result, I kept the group together. It was taking hours to get down. When it started getting closer to dark, I thought "I have to make a decision here." So, I stayed with the three as we continued our descent and sent the two sound companions down to camp to come back with assistance, warm clothing, food and hot drink, because I knew that hypothermia and shock were significant factors.

By the time darkness was approaching, the rescue party had come up with the warm clothing and equipment. Once they got to me, I explained all the things that happened and then I had to take care of myself. I left the injured people with the rescue party and went down because I needed hot drinks, food and rest to get my mind and body together.

End of Scenario

The Expert's Reflections ...

I've been down enough snow slopes in the summer so going into that basin I knew that if I felt it was unsafe, I could have retreated. Crossing the basin to that far left hand margin, I gained confidence in the snow. It wasn't knee deep in slush and things weren't breaking away, so after my first 100 steps, I felt quite confident that I was doing the right thing.

I wanted to stay out of the centre and remain on the edge because it wouldn't be a major trigger area. That was the safest way to go. As I plunge stepped down the slope, the mid-calf deep snow didn't really change, which is normal for that time of the year, and there wasn't any problem with the people on the rope behind me.

You deal with the problem when it arises. I knew nothing about these people's skill levels, so I took the safest rather than most direct way.

I didn't know what their ability was on snow, and I didn't know their reasoning processes. It was surprising that the three decided amongst themselves not to follow what I had recommended.

I mean you don't sit there as a Drill Sergeant saying, "Hey, you do this, you do that." I tried to be friendly. At the same time, I was trying to be clear saying, "Here's the situation. Here's what to do." I gave them what I thought were adequate instructions. The fact that they decided not to plunge step was beyond my control. Afterwards I asked why they decided to glissade. They said they thought it would be fun.

As I led down the left side of the basin, we were walking close enough to the edge so that if it avalanched, we could have exited onto the rock and would be safe.

I was quite familiar with the mountain snowpack, and I've done many glissades. My longest was a thousand vertical feet off the south side of Mount Aberdeen on six inches of corn snow with a solid base, using our ice axes for braking and steering and the snow slope ended on a smooth runout.

Summer snow conditions can vary greatly though, as another time in the Yukon within a matter of 100 meters we went from boot top to mid thigh. We retreated off that incline and spent the whole night sitting on a rock ledge with the hope that the snow would firm up overnight. Our bivouac was cold but we climbed further up the mountain the next morning and then down safely.

To glissade safely, you should have snow (not too deep) supported by a good solid base so that if you fall, you can self-arrest. The snow in the basin was too deep and wet to glissade, that's why I chose to plunge step down the edge. I can't think of a time when I glissaded roped to someone else. That was not a good decision.

In the winter the snow is different of course, but the same thinking applies - you are always looking for data. For example, I use the ski pole test regularly. By pushing your ski pole down into the snow, you can feel the hardness of the layers, similar to the finger/fist test in a snow pit.

Another method is the pie test. When you ski tour up into steep terrain, you make a kick turn on the switch back. As you get up over the track below, you jump in place to see how the layers react. If the corner comes off, that's good information regarding the layers and similar to a Rutsch block test in the snow pit.

Top tips to others? I guess the big C word, communication. Along the way, talk so you know what the second rope is going to do. Once I got out of communication range down at the bottom, I couldn't talk to them. By stopping halfway down I could have said "Hey, just to repeat, this is what we're doing." That's really what caused the accident - a lack of communication.

I should have spent more time talking to them. We may have picked a different objective in the morning once I understood their lack of fitness and or lack of mountaineering skills.

Be persistent in communication. Just know that people can ignore you. I was once with two experts who were leading a party in touchy conditions and despite their expertise, they still got it wrong. That's why when we get into avalanche terrain, it's worth having a group discussion. Don't make decisions on your own. Be careful of the guys with a macho attitude who tend to charge ahead.

People end up making poor decisions, like glissading down the basin roped together, because they are scared or overconfident. You need a fair amount of experience to make the proper decision.

I think mentorship is extremely important. I was so fortunate. My mentors gave me a very, very solid background. I also think a lot of my confidence was built up through experience where I had to make a lot of important decisions that saved incidents and lives.

I have had PTSD through a chain of events until I went for professional help. These included surviving a size 5 avalanche, being a first responder in a very serious ski accident and having a student die of a heart attack despite my CPR attempts.

But I eventually realized that I did the best that I could. It is hard because you are thinking "should've, would've, could've." When you get into that kind of situation, it just destroys you.

What I cannot control is the actions of others, in the mountains or on the highways.

Safety has always been my rule number one. I wasn't up there just for fun. I was out there to make sure everybody got up and down safely.

"Mountaineering is the art of going safely in dangerous places".

End of the Expert's Reflections

What are the five key points you developed?

Key Points Generated by ChatGPT-4

Note: OpenAI has attached the following to its webpage "ChatGPT can make mistakes. Check important info." Do you agree with what has been summarized?

Route Assessment and Decision Making:

Prioritize safety by avoiding steep, unstable terrain, especially in wet snow conditions. Understand that the middle of a snow basin can be highly dangerous due to potential wet snow avalanches and underlying water hazards.

Constantly evaluate snow conditions and adjust the plan accordingly. Opt for safer routes, such as edges of basins, where the risk of triggering avalanches is lower.

Importance of Communication:

Maintain clear, continuous communication with the group to ensure everyone understands and follows instructions. Frequent check-ins, especially when out of direct sight, are crucial.

Ensure that all members are aware of the potential dangers and the rationale behind chosen routes and techniques. Clarify procedures and expectations to prevent misjudgments.

Team Management and Safety Protocols:

When leading a group, especially with varying skill levels, use techniques like short roping to manage and safeguard inexperienced members.

Stagger group movements to minimize risk exposure and ensure that the leader can monitor and correct actions as needed.

Emergency Response and Rescue Readiness:

Be prepared for emergency scenarios, such as avalanches, by understanding rescue techniques. Ensure the group has the necessary equipment and knowledge for self-rescue. Stay vigilant and ready to adapt plans swiftly in response to changing conditions and unexpected group behavior.

Learning and Mentorship:

Emphasize the value of continuous learning and experience. Encourage novice technicians to seek mentorship and gain diverse field experiences to build confidence and decision-making skills. Reflect on experiences and learn from past incidents to improve future safety and efficiency in mountaineering and avalanche response.

In team decision making I say "Argue like you are right, listen like you are wrong, and be prepared the change your perspective at any time."

Cake Walk – changing conditions and plans

Read the following scenario developed from an interview with an expert and stop at the decision point question as indicated by the statement...

"Write down your cues, goals, and what are you thinking/doing."

The following is very important and is how you will learn using this method.

Put yourself in the place of the expert and write down what you would be thinking and or doing if you were in that situation. **If you don't take the time to do this... you won't learn.**

Note that the information in the scenario might be incomplete, much the same as it would be in the real world.

<u>Do not skip ahead</u>. Reading ahead to see what the expert has done before you have put your thoughts down, will negate the value of this exercise.

After you have put your thoughts on paper refer to the next page "Thoughts of the Expert...". Have you differed or missed something? Think about that.

Continue reading the scenario sections, writing down your thoughts, and reading those of the expert until you come to the end. Reflect about the situation. In the same position, would you make the same decisions? What would be the outcome of those decisions?

Read the Expert's reflections to gain context and deeper understanding.

During your review of the expert's scenario and their thoughts, write down 5 key points. Compare your 5 to those developed by ChatGPT-4.

If you have any questions or comments, please reach out to
helicourse@gmail.com

Cake Walk 1

It is February and you are the leading two groups in a multi machine, helicopter skiing operation with limited tree skiing. You are looking at a pretty stormy week and this is a window of reasonable weather. The weather is changing and throughout the day will increasingly limit the visibility up high. During the morning guides meeting the plan has been developed that with 6 groups and three helicopters, you will start with Alpha, a small, very familiar mellow run about 1500' long that is above tree line but not high into the alpine. On the avalanche rating scale it is rated challenging because of its multiple rolls some of which are quite steep. It has a variable slope angle with low angle on the right, steepening to the left.

Alpha doesn't have a history of avalanche activity and is skied quite a bit because it is close to the lodge. On the flight out you fly past Bravo and notice it has had some kind of natural avalanche. This is very surprising. Although steeper terrain than Alpha, it's more of a basin with a vertical wall above that shelters it from the wind and it looks like maybe a cornice or something overhead has triggered the slide. It is a large, probably a size 2, larger than what you expect on such a small feature.

You land on Alpha and ski with the group down the first shallow pitch. It is much windier and maybe a bit warmer than you have anticipated, and there is a really cakey wind slab. It doesn't feel like what you had expected - a more "regular" feeling wind slab that is cold snow, and is either harder to penetrate with skis due to firmness, or a lighter, less dense wind slab that is easy to turn through.

The very top pitch of the run feels pretty good with no surface hoar. When you get off the glacier it steepens and there is a little bit more down flow or cross loading wind effect.

(1). Write down your cues, goals, and what are you thinking/doing.

<u>Do not skip ahead</u>

Thoughts and Actions of the Expert 1

We were trying to spread the helicopters out which was a challenge due to the limited terrain caused by the weather. So, the plan was to ski what we could get to in the alpine, go out to the farthest runs until the weather chased us back to below tree line.

We landed on the shoulder of Alpha and I was doing what I think of as the proper due diligence, starting out on the right side less steep side of the run.

The pitch below the glacier didn't feel quite right, it was spongier, cakier. There was a change in snow density, hard to read in flat light and it wasn't so much how the pitch felt as how the whole situation felt: first run of the day, maybe the first time out in a couple of days, noting an abnormal avalanche observation, it was just a feeling that I should take it easier and slower than usual.

Seeing the avalanche on Bravo and feeling the snow under my feet as different from my expectations was making me slowly decide that I'm going to ski this differently than I normally would. I don't know why, but there was a thought in my head of like, I'm gonna go ski this and leave the group here, then I will call them down on the radio.

I left the group in a place that I would probably normally park people. Generally we're looking for a bench above a steep pitch where guests can regroup above the avalanche terrain but still be able to see the guide in front of them. An abnormal regroup would be all together on a steep pitch where the combined load of people increases the likelihood of triggering deeper layers of concern.

Alpha is a run that you would typically just ski altogether because in heliskiing if you can't put one person on the slope because of avalanche danger, you can't justify putting the whole group on it. So then you just don't ski it.

I ski probably 150 feet, not very far at all, when I hear them shouting at me. I stopped on the next little bench to see what's going on. I had essentially remoted the entire feature. The fracture initiated between us across the entire run and went from above me but below them.

From the simplest side on the right it went all the way over to the steepest side of the run, probably size 2 1/2, stopping just shy of the helicopter pickup.

This was something that the other guides, who have been working at the company for a long time, have never seen happen before. They were always curious if a slide on Alpha could take out the pickup. I can say with full confidence that if it'd just been a little bit thicker, a little bit more mass, then for sure it would have done so. And if you get taken off the pickup, then it's 1500 meters to the valley floor through really nasty huge country below you.

If I had guided a little bit differently, it would have involved people. The line that we were on was the less severe line and it was not the main body of the avalanche, but it would have resulted in guest involvement to some extent. It definitely would have buried and killed people.

Cake Walk 2

A helicopter with the lead guide flies up the valley, headed towards the adjacent run, Charlie.

(2). Write down your cues, goals, and what are you thinking/doing.

<u>Do not skip ahead</u>

Thoughts and of the Expert 2

I radioed the lead guide when I hear where they're going. and call him off. I said "Yeah, we can't ski this (because of the slide). We cannot be skiing Charlie (because it is similar to Alpha and Bravo). We have to pull way back. Things are happening that we didn't foresee.

That call ended up being kind of a critical point in the season overall, as the guide in the front seat of that helicopter was new to the company. Not new to guiding, not new to heliskiing at all, just new to the terrain. He felt really responsible for the fact that now he was flying around and his Plan A was thrown out the window. I said over the radio for all to hear that you can't go based on what we're seeing in the last 15 minutes. I know it's open on the run list, but I don't think we can ski that run today.

I really felt that he thought he was being undermined, getting the carpet ripped out. It obviously wasn't a personal thing but he saw it that way. He took it upon himself in a way that was difficult for him. That day kind of really set the tone. We had to work together and here I am telling him he can't ski that run. For the rest of the season we had to work together.

I've never actually called someone on the radio regarding an open run and said, "We shouldn't be skiing this based on what I'm seeing here." So yeah, he might not have appreciated it, but in the end we just ended up going to a lower elevation and skiing in the trees with all the groups in just two helicopters. It totally changed the plan for the day based on, you know, a pretty close call in the morning.

End of Scenario

The Expert's Reflections ...

We were thinking the weather is coming in, it is going to deteriorate, so let's start with Alpha and then as the day goes on we will get pushed out of those places anyway, which is a totally valid plan. So consciously or not we were just kind of let's go for all the gold we can before the visibility or weather deteriorates (snowing or low ceiling). When that happens we're going to get pushed down into the zones that we can still ski.

I was scared. Things were super touchy. Calling off the lead guide was the knee jerk reaction to seeing this totally unexpected result and not really understanding how or why it happened. Rather than trying to analyze it, the knee jerk reaction was just let's pull the pin on this zone and go somewhere else. The plan completely changed for the day. So, instead of trying to process it and stay close to the line, I said, "You know what, there's danger here. Let's just leave the zone."

It's always hard to know if the danger is isolated only to that run and so I just completely called him off. That was probably a bit of an overreaction, but I don't know. He was heading to a bigger, more planar feature that produces a larger avalanche. We saw it on A. We saw it on B. Now C is right next door, and we are going to ski that?

I am kind of a curious person. I was definitely riding that line between the green side of the run and the blue side of the run, trying to get on to some terrain that is a little bit steeper to see how reactive it was. I definitely achieved that.

The fracture line wasn't super deep, probably 50 centimeters, certainly deep enough. I think that's what it was, just new snow and warm temps. It ended up being a really small layer of facets that were just particularly reactive.

When you look at the photos of the slide with us on the hill, you see these little specks of us standing on the slope on these islands that hadn't slid, but everything around us has ripped out.

I usually don't think I'll just hike out of a run if I don't like it. There has to be a number of things that kind of go not quite right to find myself walking back up. In the past I have ignored that nagging voice that says I shouldn't land on this run and then I'm out of the machine, it has flown away and I have some time to really think about it. I'm ignoring calling the machine back up, so I'm going to at least poke in a little. And then there's the potential that even after looking a little bit, I'm going to continue to ignore that sense of "I don't think I want to bring other humans into this situation."

For me it is two strikes not three, and you're out. I want to feel that things align with my expectations and when they do I feel really confident about decision making. Sometimes things don't feel right, such as it's difficult to see the texture of the snow from the air because it's flat light and the snow feels different under foot than I expected I think maybe it's just on the ridge. So I will ski a few turns onto the feature to get a sense of does it improve? Does it deteriorate? It doesn't take much, it just takes a couple of things that don't quite line up with my expectations. Then those sirens go off pretty quick for me.

In the past I sometimes totally ignored what I should have been looking for as I was thinking, "Well, So and so did it so I guess I have to follow." Or I watched the other guides open up this line this way so many times under similar conditions.

There's generally a default mode which is really important for, I think, managing risk. It's basically operating without thinking hard about what you're doing, like when you drive your car from point A to B, arriving at B and realizing you don't fully remember the drive up to that point. Default mode allows you to think about many things simultaneously rather than focusing on one at a time, it's a generally comfortable place to be where things feel "normal" or "as they should." You can make good decisions in a standard setting.

This default mode of risk management allows you to manage a ton of variables all at the same time. That being said, you have to be open to the aberrations that trigger the siren.

You need to put the whole ski day in context, the whole week, the whole season and to make that repeatable season after season. I'm no longer thinking just about my day, my week, my season, my company. I'm also thinking about the state of the industry overall. Good decisions or safety, that's not a currency that you can bank. You can't say well we've been safe all season for 90% of the time so we can go hang it out for 10. It doesn't obviously work that way at all.

I've seen new lead guides with a numbered list, planning to ski this run and this run, then this run, and that run. This itinerary for the day has a lot of thought put into it but as they get familiar with the terrain, they find it is better to have a very loose plan. Kind of pick a direction and start flying that way.

The risk of doing the homework at the lodges is getting too committed to your initial plan. And you know, the reality is that's what happened to me on Run X despite seeing that recent activity on Run Y. In retrospect, the right thing to do would have been a 180 right then and there and just flown back to some of the tree runs.

The problem in sticking to the plan is I think you're committing to having blinders on in a sense. You're no longer looking for observations. You already made the decision, so now you're looking for confirmation of that decision.

I think we should be comfortable with the discomfort of indecision. Not indecision, as that sounds wishy washy, but be comfortable with that uncertainty. Then you're not looking for information for or against a particular outcome, you're just generally looking for information, which for me keeps my head on a swivel to see what else there is.

I'm looking at every place else that I could never ski because there could be indications there. I'm not focused on the run, on the run quality. I'm looking at all the other things like overhead cornices and recent wind direction.

Some inexperienced ski guides are so focused on the guests and group control that they stop doing things like regrouping. They will continue skiing and call back on the radio instead of stopping and regrouping. This shows that they aren't adapting to the change in the situation as they are focused on the skiers and not necessarily focused on the terrain.

I'm always going to stop above a hazard even if I didn't know it was there. New guides sometimes devote lot more attention to the client experience (which is really important) but at the end of the day, the client experience I'm most concerned with is their safety.

Observations need to be shared with the team in the moment. There's no "I will share that when I get back to the lodge at the end of the day." The rule is that pertinent information has to go out to everybody right away.

I am constantly in that struggle of how do we calibrate our collective mindset. So when we say we're status quo, we're stepping back, stepping out, everyone needs to have the same definition of what that means i.e. this is what it looks like in the field.

Many times there might not be good options, but at least there are options. I think the novice is going to be more likely to face a situation where it's like go or no go but I think the expert is constantly in the process of creating options. The third way.

I wouldn't say that anything is like safe, you know, I don't use that terminology.

End of the Expert's Reflections

What are the five key points you developed?

Key Points Generated by ChatGPT-4

Note: OpenAI has attached the following to its webpage "ChatGPT can make mistakes. Check important info." Do you agree with what has been summarized?

Adapting to Unexpected Conditions:

Observation: Always be vigilant and adaptable to changing conditions. The wind slab and unexpected snow behavior on Alpha indicated potential instability.

Response: If something feels off, such as snow behaving unexpectedly or visual signs of instability, reassess your plan immediately. Don't hesitate to change the plan, even if it disrupts the day's schedule.

Communication and Team Safety:

Communication: Clearly and promptly communicate observations and concerns to the entire team. For example, calling off skiing Charlie after observing instability on Alpha and Bravo was crucial.

Decision-Making: Ensure all guides are on the same page. Publicly discussing concerns helps in making informed decisions and maintaining collective safety.

Terrain Management:

Terrain Familiarity: Use familiar, less steep terrain when conditions are uncertain. Starting on the right side of Alpha, which was less steep, demonstrated caution.

Parking and Spacing: Place groups in safe zones and always stop above potential hazards. Parking in a safe location allows for reassessment and avoids exposure to potential avalanche paths.

Risk Assessment and Response:

On-the-Fly Assessment: Continuously evaluate the terrain and conditions while skiing. The decision to ski a few turns and then re-evaluate is crucial for understanding current snow stability.

Emergency Protocols: Be prepared for emergency scenarios, such as triggering an unexpected avalanche. Understand that leaving the group in a safe spot and skiing down to assess the slope can prevent group involvement in an avalanche.

Experience and Judgment:

Trusting Instincts: Trust your instincts and experience. If something feels wrong, act on it. The decision to ski cautiously and reassess was based on a gut feeling that proved correct.

Continuous Learning: Learn from each experience and be open to adapting your methods. Reflect on past decisions, both right and wrong, to improve future risk management strategies.

The White Canvas – buried layers and triggers

Read the following scenario developed from an interview with an expert and stop at the decision point question as indicated by the statement...

"Write down your cues, goals, and what are you thinking/doing."

The following is very important and is how you will learn using this method.

Put yourself in the place of the expert and write down what you would be thinking and or doing if you were in that situation. **If you don't take the time to do this... you won't learn.**

Note that the information in the scenario might be incomplete, much the same as it would be in the real world.

<u>Do not skip ahead</u>. Reading ahead to see what the expert has done before you have put your thoughts down, will negate the value of this exercise.

After you have put your thoughts on paper refer to the next page "Thoughts of the Expert...". Have you differed or missed something? Think about that.

Continue reading the scenario sections, writing down your thoughts, and reading those of the expert until you come to the end. Reflect about the situation. In the same position, would you make the same decisions? What would be the outcome of those decisions?

Read the Expert's reflections to gain context and deeper understanding.

During your review of the expert's scenario and their thoughts, write down 5 key points. Compare your 5 to those developed by ChatGPT-4.

If you have any questions or comments, please reach out to
helicourse@gmail.com

The White Canvas 1

You are the avalanche control professional on a large project in the Coast Mountains. The crew are working on a powerline above treeline, digging out the towers' guy wires, some by machine, some by hand. Snowcats are building roads into the towers and you have been asked to do avalanche safety on a tower that is located below a slope with the biggest potential for creating an avalanche. You have built this road before and know it isn't difficult to build a road on the slope, however there's a problem with a buried surface hoar layer.

You are lucky enough to be able to sit in with the local heliski guides during their meetings and listen to them discuss this layer. They have determined that it is still noted as a problem but skier triggering is considered very unlikely. You go onto the slope to the tower and dig a profile at the guy wire, which is a slightly different aspect than the main start zone. You think it is a good spot because it has to be dug out by hand anyway and you might as well give the crew a head start. The surface hoar is found but testing produces inconsistent hard resistant planar results.

You agree with the cat driver that the road can be dug out today and you will ride with him down to the tower. You bring the other snowcat up to the top of the slope as a backup. This cat driver has worked all winter digging out roads in places with no avalanche danger. You also bring the hand laborers from the other side up to the top to be available.

(1). Write down your cues, goals, and what are you thinking/doing.

<u>Do not skip ahead</u>

Thoughts and Actions of the Expert 1

The fact that the layer was not skier triggerable anymore gave me a little seed of confirmation bias, that it was not going to be a problem. I was not really connecting that the ski guides were looking at the hazard from skiers traveling over terrain. I should have been looking at it from the fact that I'm going to put in a cat road that might be digging into the layer. I was thinking that even if we triggered an avalanche, I'm sure that the most it would do is maybe push the cat.

I thought we had safety backup with the other cat on top of the slope except I didn't really think about the fact that the cat driver had almost zero avalanche experience. He's up there as backup, but nobody's told him what his new task entails. He just knows he has to be there.

He is just sitting around, but he wants to do something. He decides he's going to start digging out the tower that is in the avalanche path above us.

So while we are making the road below, he digs down and through the surface hoar layer, and he sees a shooting crack go right in front of his blade. He triggered the slope right above us and it ran down in front of our cat. It was a near miss.

I didn't think we were going to trigger the slope from the toe because the start zone is mostly confined to an area that is above a bit of a cliff and is not connected to where the road goes. But, if somebody had asked me, "Do you think you could trigger the start zone by penetrating and disturbing the weak layer?" Yeah, absolutely it's a possibility.

I was thinking about it afterwards, what created this incident. The biggest single thing was that we changed our tasks for the day. We didn't group everybody together and say, "OK, this is the new task and here are your roles and responsibilities. These are the hazards associated with this task. We are not doing what we're normally doing. We are doing a different thing, which is opening this road so your job is this now, not that." Make them understand that we've got a different approach.

That ends up being a bit of a lack of situational awareness on my part because I just assumed that they understood when we said, "You're going to be on the top in case something happens." I never said, "Don't continue working like you normally would work."

I was only one who had the backup helicopter frequencies on my radio. We hadn't gone over the Emergency rescue plan. Like "What if something happens here, who would you call?" The crew wouldn't have had the phone numbers for the local heli operator or anything. So even though we had an emergency response plan, it was sitting on the shelf back in town.

I had tunnel vision about opening the road and the safety of the one cat, but not keeping the situational awareness what else might be going on around me.

Everybody needs to know what to do if something happens. You can't be making assumptions that everybody is on the same page that you are. Our safety margin is also built on our ability to respond quickly. If you just assume it's there, well, we know that doesn't work.

Your entire margin of safety is built on your ability to recognize all of the potential risk factors and doing your best to mitigate them. Make sure you cover it all, think through the "what ifs". If this goes badly, then what?

You can make some assumptions that people understand what we understand, but they don't necessarily. We have had trouble in the guiding industry where guides internalize all of the risks and then there's an incident. People say "We had no idea we were exposing ourselves to that kind of risk. We weren't involved in the decision making or we didn't even talk about it. Remember, people are part of the team, right?

Success is fundamentally unstable and remains so because of the dynamic nature of change, instability, and flexibility.

The White Canvas 2

It is now spring-time and the contractor wants to open a road over a pass buried by 6 metres of snow. It is on the north facing side of the valley underneath a gentle slope with a start zone quite a bit above it. In mid-winter this area is subject to larger avalanches from the upper start zone. The avalanche forecast for today has this north facing slope open for work with an unlikely probability of triggering avalanches. Across the valley, the steep south facing slope is closed due to an increased potential for avalanches with solar input and daytime warming.

The contractor has excavators digging the road out and has become very concerned about an avalanche threat from the 6 metre high snow walls they are creating above the machines, not avalanches from the slope above. It is the beginning of spring and there have been several melt freeze cycles and the temperatures are well below zero overnight. They want you to do something to protect the workers in the machines.

(2). Write down your cues, goals, and what are you thinking/doing.

Do not skip ahead

Thoughts and Actions of the Expert 2

The contractors had very little snow experience. Suddenly they can see this 6 metre wall dramatically showing them the huge amount of snow, and they say "Oh that's super dangerous. We are digging this thing out and you're the rescue guy. We want somebody to sit here and watch out for the crew." So that's what we did, parked a couple of techs in a truck with Starlink for 12 hours a day. Nothing happened.

That's an example of people looking at it from two different perspectives, where one side doesn't really understand the process.

It's a coastal snowpack in spring. Solid rounds straight to the ground. Yes, they're digging in it, but it's doesn't have any specific weak layers and is not isothermal. It's a solid block of frozen snow stable enough that you can basically cut the bottom out of it out with the an excavator and not have it slide down on top.

That sort of stuff, parking the techs, was like "Well we don't do it that way. That's what the forecast is for." We wouldn't have let the excavators in there if we didn't think there was a very low risk of anything coming down because they are basically just digging out a snow drift in the spring. The excavator operators are wearing beacons and have training and have a very low vulnerability because they are sitting in a 40 tonne piece of machinery with cages over the windows.

Our confidence in the forecast came from many bags of Anfo (explosives), digging, and the absence of any avalanche activity on shaded aspects like the one they were on. So we go, "OK. We bombed the heck out of this basically homogenous chunk of snow that doesn't have any surface problems on it. We're well into the spring melt freeze where you know, it's frozen. It's just not moving." So you build yourself up to a level of confidence by testing.

The days were not yet hot enough to create a glide slab or go isothermal and we were doing daily checks and observations to confirm that. It takes a long time to actually create isothermal conditions where it's loose and flowing like slush. You would need to watch out for glide cracks on a steep slope where you might have water running down on a rock slab. Had there been a deep persistent weak layer, that might have changed the confidence level.

That south facing side of the valley we had closed or conditionally opened it. That's where your forecasts are important. For example, knowing you can go in there in the morning, but with no workers on foot or only teams of two exposing themselves one at a time with avalanche training and PPE. Those kinds of mitigations would be for that one spot.

In opening up the road, you have a guy sitting in a 40 tonne excavator digging the slope that doesn't have anything above it, so you know the worst that could happen is maybe a block of snow could fall over on him. But he is not very vulnerable inside an excavator.

"If you are considering only 2 options, find at least one more." Shane Parrish

The White Canvas 3

In a different location in late spring, an environmental crew wants to fly into one of the side valleys and do some stream sampling. This location has a deep persistent weak layer that is becoming an avalanche problem as the heat penetrates and free water reaches the deep buried crust/facet layer. You know there's potential for full path runout because the heat was getting at the snowpack causing deep slab releases. There have been several very large avalanches over the last few hot days. You are not doing avalanche control up the valley but just basically monitoring the conditions on these slopes as they do not affect the work area.

You take the helicopter and go look at the spot they want to sample and determine there is no avalanche hazard there. The helicopter takes the crew out and drops them off.

An hour later another helicopter pilot flying farther up the valley from the stream sampling crew and with whom you have built up a relationship of information sharing, calls you and says a very large slide has come down farther up the drainage and blocked the river.

(2). Write down your cues, goals, and what are you thinking/doing.
<u>Do not skip ahead</u>

Thoughts and Actions of the Expert 3

We were starting to see some very large slides happen with really hot days and warm nights. The pilot said it blocked the river. Then I go, "OK, well, that's kind of interesting. That's a pretty big avalanche." And then it took like probably 30 seconds for the penny to drop.

Well if it blocked the river and those guys are downstream, what's going to happen when it unblocks? I had better call them.

So it's sort of a subsequent hazard to the actual avalanche hazard. That is one of the things that normally goes through my thought process now. The river had stopped flowing above where they're doing samples. They were finished and were about to leave when I called. When the river did penetrate the debris dam, the resulting lake let loose and flooded the area where they were sampling.

I think the problem was with my perception of what could be a risk to them related only to avalanches. I was stuck with my own paradigm of what would be directly at risk if an avalanche were to come down. Would the crew be in a runout zone? I did not consider the further potential risk if a large avalanche were to come down and block the river. I never went there in my mind.

We sometimes get stuck in our decision making frameworks that work most of the time. But when you have unusual things, maybe you just have to say, hey, this is really unusual. Is there something about this I'm missing? (which I was).

If you recognize that you're subject to bias, then you might be able to pull yourself back at some point to say, am I making this decision objectively, or is my bias pushing me into this because I want it to happen?

End of Scenario

The Expert's Reflections ...

A thing about the canvas of snow is that sometimes we don't understand as instructors what the student is seeing or not seeing. That is quite eye opening because you can have some assumptions people are getting it but were actually not seeing the same thing that you were seeing. They just aren't perceiving the terrain or the snow on the terrain the same way.

They can get themselves into trouble because they simply can't visualize terrain in a way that puts them into it in a kind of harmonious way which allows them to move through terrain and accept the avalanche hazard on a given day.

Some people are very analytical. They need to have checkboxes but they don't necessarily put it together into a bigger picture, whereas other people just kind of see it.

There's all of these subtleties that generate the layers that create the problems on the white canvas. They are the details of the painting. You need to be able to think about the characteristics of the terrain's snowpack that have been created by the winter's weather events.

You're looking at the whole picture, but you're also looking at the subtleties, the clues that the terrain is giving you. For example, the very subtle differences in slope angle, wind loading, and aspect can create quite a difference in the snowpack. You need to put the snow on top of the terrain. How thick is it in a certain area relative to wind? Is there wind loading somewhere? Is there a layer that is preserved in a shaded place that isn't in another spot? I think that comes with conscious situational awareness.

If I am going to go to somewhere I haven't been, I start to track the weather from early in the season. You can then arrive with a predetermined understanding of what kind of snowpack you expect to find based on the weather patterns of that particular area. You are already further down the road than if you just arrived there and say, "OK, now I'm going to try with this blank slate and start to fill in all the all the problems." It's not that you know everything when you get there, it's just that you do have a sense of what you expect to find and then you can build on that.

We all have different risk tolerance, but we also have different ways of making decisions. Some people are more prone to an accident or an incident. That is just based on your own character. So once you recognize that it's a weakness in your character you can slow down little bit, reflect and say "Is this me doing what I normally do?"

You still have to make a choice about hazard and maybe recognize that you are subject to bias. Yeah, none of us are free from it. We can try to be objective. If you recognize that you're subject to bias, then you might be able to pull yourself back at some point to say," Am I making this objectively or is my bias pushing me into this because I want it to happen?

You know, I'm not against having a structure that makes people think. It can be a problem if they do it by rote without understanding the purpose of having this rule. Why do we have this procedure here? And it's usually because there was a previous incident or accident where people said, "Well, we've got to make a way for people to make the decision that's going to prevent that from happening in the future."

We know the way to solve a lot accidents. First of all by design, so it can't happen. That's better than having to say we recognize it can happen but now you're going to have a rule that prevents you from doing the wrong thing.

But remember that harsh learning environments and dynamic environments require high level expertise to get the job done. That's where simple rules might not always work because you have to be nimble enough to be able to adapt quickly and not fall back on a rule based system but actually say "Hey I know what needs to be done here, I'll do it right now." That solves the problem.

You know, when things are unusual, then unusual things happen.

When recognizing that conditions are outside the normal you basically don't fall back on your normal expectations of size or consequence. You increase your safety margin.

In an avalanche career unusual events happen to us but in that span you don't get to see it all. You may never see one of those seasons where you have this giant 100 year event. So recognize what it is you don't know. You can only be so certain. And one of the things that you learn as you go is the greater your uncertainty, the greater your margin of safety has to be.

The avalanche experts, so-called avalanche experts, they're the ones that are picking their way down the side of the slide path. Giving themselves a safe out, knowing that they don't really know that much. The other guys are centre punching it.

So start with the big picture important stuff. We know it's a nuanced field where there's lots of detail that helps to fill in where it might be tricky or not.

Experienced avalanche forecasters have the ability to look at a whole bunch of different factors that would create avalanche problems for the day. They can filter out what is not important and can hone in on what is.

When you're new, it's all there. You are getting all this information. What does it mean? It is difficult if you don't have the framework to put it together. As we get into this world where there's so much information available, it's sometimes easier to actually take in less.

We base our terrain choices on where we know it's safe. Where we are uncertain, we have to decide if we we're going there or not based on filling in our knowledge gaps or doing more testing. We take in a lot of information with our eyes, our skis, and walking along the snow and looking and seeing. It doesn't have to be written in a notebook. We have lots of sensors, so if you're paying attention, just traveling in a terrain can often give you the answers you need.

One thing experienced people will have that novices don't is they will either have been directly involved in or associated with the downside or the consequence side of the risk decision making things. We're always talking about the reward side. You know, it's going to be great. We're going to get this. But we don't really think about the downside of those pluses, of taking risks. When that does go wrong, what does that really mean? What's a consequence? When you have these accidents or incidents, it can be life altering for people. It definitely helps you to understand what the downside could be.

How do you recognize your biases? Am I really thinking about what could go wrong here? Maybe make it a little more balanced decision, about what level of risk you're going to put yourself through.

End of the Expert's Reflections

What are the five key points you developed?

Key Points Generated by ChatGPT-4

Note: OpenAI has attached the following to its webpage "ChatGPT can make mistakes. Check important info." Do you agree with what has been summarized?

Understand the Risk of Buried Layers:

Recognize that even if a surface hoar layer is no longer skier-triggerable, it can still pose a significant risk when disturbed by heavy machinery like snowcats. Always evaluate the potential for triggering an avalanche when altering the snowpack, especially by digging or creating roads. Identify biases and ensure that decisions are based on current data and comprehensive risk assessments, not assumptions or past experiences alone.

Clear Communication and Task Assignment:

Ensure that all team members are aware of their specific roles and the potential risks involved. Before changing tasks or procedures, gather the team and communicate the new plan clearly, including any changes in risk and safety measures.

Training and Situational Awareness:

All team members, including those providing backup, need adequate avalanche training and situational awareness. They should understand what to look for and how to respond in an emergency. Never assume that everyone has the same level of understanding.

Balancing Risk and Safety:

Experienced avalanche technicians leverage their understanding of snow and terrain to make informed decisions. They balance the risks and rewards, ensuring safety margins are adjusted according to uncertainties, and rely on structured procedures and situational awareness to guide actions.

Continued...

Managing Unusual Hazards:

Novel or unexpected situations, such as potential downstream flooding from an avalanche blocking a river, require a flexible and adaptive approach. Recognizing and addressing biases in decision-making can help foresee and mitigate secondary hazards.

"A person is extremely uncomfortable with uncertainty. To deal with his discomfort, man tends to create a false sense of security by substituting certainty for uncertainty." Bennett, W Goodspeed.

Mother's Surprise – Risk, Instincts, and survival in snow

Read the following scenario developed from an interview with an expert and stop at the decision point question as indicated by the statement...

"Write down your cues, goals, and what are you thinking/doing."

The following is very important and is how you will learn using this method.

Put yourself in the place of the expert and write down what you would be thinking and or doing if you were in that situation. **If you don't take the time to do this... you won't learn.**

Note that the information in the scenario might be incomplete, much the same as it would be in the real world.

<u>Do not skip ahead</u>. Reading ahead to see what the expert has done before you have put your thoughts down, will negate the value of this exercise.

After you have put your thoughts on paper refer to the next page "Thoughts of the Expert...". Have you differed or missed something? Think about that.

Continue reading the scenario sections, writing down your thoughts, and reading those of the expert until you come to the end. Reflect about the situation. In the same position, would you make the same decisions? What would be the outcome of those decisions?

Read the Expert's reflections to gain context and deeper understanding.

During your review of the expert's scenario and their thoughts, write down 5 key points. Compare your 5 to those developed by ChatGPT-4.

If you have any questions or comments, please reach out to
helicourse@gmail.com

If it is on your mind it is worth mentioning

Mother's Surprise 1

You are an assistant guide working your first season at a heliski company in eastern BC. It is mid-winter and the snowpack has some fairly large depth hoar buried at the bottom, with a 1finger midpack, large surface hoar on top of midpack, and a final layer of low density snow on top.

The managers have closed some runs, telling everyone to stay away from a particular angle of slope that is maybe only 10° steeper than the open runs, for 3 or 4 days to let the snowpack settle down. You arrive with your group on top of this small, slightly steeper type of slope, exactly what the managers have been telling you about. It is maybe only five or six turns in a little bowl.

(1). Write down your cues, goals, and what are you thinking/doing.

Do not skip ahead

Thoughts and Actions of the Expert 1

Of course, being a young guide like I was and being full of testosterone and ego, I came across this slope with my group and didn't think anything of it. I didn't realize at the time that this was the small slope I was not supposed to ski. So I told the clients as I normally would, give me two or three turns and then you follow me.

I was into my third turn and the slope let go. I was looking down at the bottom of the small bowl-like feature to see the snow taking me towards the trees. So I clicked off my skis, got rid of my poles, and took my pack off. I used the pack as a device to ferry across the slope, kind of body surfing by leaning on it then spinning over it, then moving the pack over my body, then leaning on it again, and repeat. I stopped a fair ways to the side and above the trees but the client that was three turns behind me ended up nose to nose to a tree. If I hadn't used the pack in that way, I would have been pushed down through the timber.

I could have been seriously injured. I had always thought about the safety part right from the beginning but I didn't really understand the snow in-stability aspect at that time.

When the last storm came in and put low density snow on top of the surface hoar, that raised a lot of red flags as the lead guide/manager had explained. I didn't understand then how important it was to stay on low angle terrain, as I was still very young and eager to please the guests.

We were having fun as a group on that day. You know, then all of a sudden you have forgotten to evaluate the whole thing because you're too inexperienced, you're enjoying what you're doing, and the guests; they're having fun. You kind of throw away the idea of the red flags around you, they just don't enter your mind.

From this, my first experience in an avalanche, I learned to be more attentive, listening to senior people who had a lot more experience than I had.

Mother's Surprise 2

You now are skiing with a class of snow studying personal mid-winter on Mt Fidelity in Rogers Pass and have an incredible snow pack. It is solid, 1 finger, pencil snowpack, at least 50 centimeters down with this new, fist density snow on the top.

You start down leading a group of students that includes another experienced tail guide. The skiing is fabulous, better than expected. You start thinking, man, this is perfect, the perfect angle, perfect snow. And you think to yourself, "OK, we've done the studies, I have the evidence for why this is stable." You think this is good to just continue straight down instead of catching the traverse to get back on the road to Fidelity.

(2). Write down your cues, goals, and what are you thinking/doing.

<u>Do not skip ahead</u>

Thoughts and Actions of the Expert 2

I thought at first, we are going to ski the upper avalanche path and do a traverse back to the Fidelity road. As we started down the avalanche path, I changed my mind. We're going to ski this slope all the way down. It was a long avalanche path. It actually comes down to the TransCanada Highway. And so we skied down and it was great. It was absolutely a magnificent day.

When we all gathered at the bottom, I said to the guide who had a number of years more experience than me, "That felt so good. I just couldn't stop." And he said "When it's good, go for it, ski it. If you feel confident and have the evidence, just do it." So that was the positive learning experience from that day, though there was no serious involvement. It definitely was a good day to ski, enjoying it without being nervous.

Mother's Surprise 3

You are back guiding heliskiing and have a good base, probably down about 20 to 25 centimeters is a really pencil hard snowpack and on top of it is a lighter low density snowpack (15-20 cms.). You know that there is some very small (0.25) surface hoar buried in between the solid snowpack and the low density new snow. The surface hoar has been buried for a week.

You are dropped off by the helicopter at the top of the run and ski down a fairly low angle slope when all of a sudden the terrain becomes quite steep (4-5 metres to the left with possible crevasse to 50 metre height to the right, all ending on a flat bench.
It had been windblown in that area over night. The snow is a little bit shallower at this lip. To the left are a series of crevasses marking the end of the glacier. On the right, the slope gets significantly steeper. There are no other terrain options that you can use to go around. Straight below you is the only option, a 10 to 12 metre slope ending in a mild terrain trap. You assess it and really believe that this slope, the only way down, is very likely going to avalanche.

(3). Write down your cues, goals, and what are you thinking/doing.
<u>Do not skip ahead</u>

Thoughts and Actions of the Expert 3

I thought, "OK, I'm in the middle of the roll over terrain at the end of a small glacier. I don't want to move the group to the left where an avalanche could push us into the crevasses and I don't want to go to the right because that's too big of a bite to take on with the buried surface hoar."

But I had to get by, so I ski cut the slope like the ski patrol would do. Nothing happened. So I started down and on my second turn I felt the slope let go, knocking my feet out from underneath me. I pushed hard on the snow, the hardpack below, and most of the snow went by me. I ended up at the bottom where the slope leveled out.

The guests wondered what had happened to me because they were just far enough back that they couldn't see me. It was a mild terrain trap, but I ended up buried maybe to my ankles, if that.

I thought to myself, OK, what? What is it I'm going to learn from this one? I knew it was going to avalanche, but I had few options. I had to commit to trying to make it safe for the clients.

I was hoping that I would ski down and maybe it would slide when I cut it at the top. But that didn't happen. It was my second turn that the slope went off but I knew it was going to happen.

I should have tried to do a vertically deeper ski cut across the lip of that particular piece of terrain. It wasn't anything different that the ski patrol would do at a ski area, cutting slopes for opening the hill. I probably didn't do a long/deep enough ski cut at the top.

End of Scenario

The Expert's Reflections ...

You cannot trust Mother Nature. You can think of all the things that you have read about and put them into practice, and Mother Nature is going to throw out a bit of something unusual; she has so many different little stories and you're not going to recognize all the clues at the time. We as human beings will not be able to comprehend all the different scenarios that she's going to throw at us.

When working in the snow/avalanche business, you're going to get caught. It is a matter of "when". It will either knock you off your feet and make you sit up and pay attention, or if you make a really big error, you will get seriously injured, or worse, it's going to be terminal for you.

It's the small incidents too, where you can run into trouble. The variation in the terrain or the way the trees have sheltered the snow when the wind was blowing can set up little scenarios that can cause you woe. Maybe there's a settlement or there's a little snow movement on a really small piece of terrain. If you ignore that, you're going to find it again sooner or later, especially if you're going to step out into something bigger. That's the nature of the business. You're not going to know everything.

If you think your day is good and you're having a real good time but you're not paying attention to the changing of things, something may happen.

Never become unaware of what is going on. Always be thinking if something happens right now, what are the consequences?

So you should find a little slope and test it out. However a negative result doesn't mean that you can then go on the big slope and be guaranteed it won't slide. Always keep thinking, what could be the consequences? If they are too great, maybe I will just go back the way I came – it won't be a fun day, but I'll go home.

Remember, keep your exposure to a minimum when testing a slope.

If there's something bothering you, it could be what they call a gut feeling. Sometimes, something just comes into your head that says "This isn't right." Slow down, take a look, and re-evaluate everything that you have thought about.

If you think there might be something not right, pick a little bit of terrain and try to figure out if you can produce a little avalanche to verify that yes, it's unstable or no, it is stable. The problem is that you won't always get a result that verifies things one way or another.

You can't prove a negative. And that's problematic because if you go through a career always skiing and having nothing happen, you think "Well I'm totally protected by angels and I can do anything I want." But sometimes the angels have to take a holiday, so you get missed that day. That's when you have your incident.

Sometimes my stomach and brain starts to send me some messages from those feelings that you get through your feet, that come up from the snow when you're skiing. If it doesn't make sense in your head and your stomach gives you a message, then maybe you'd better look again. This is a personal checkpoint for you to look at the situation completely.

God protects those that are innocent. Then you start taking avalanche courses and learning. The problem is you come out of the training going, "Oh, I have all this knowledge. Now I really know what's going on." You're not innocent anymore and God doesn't protect you, so just be aware of that. Things will happen if you're not being humble and thinking about all situations.

You do not realize how small an avalanche can be to cause you trouble. I think that's what novices don't understand. Even the smallest avalanche can cause you misfortune, knock you over, put you over cliffs, put you into trees, take you into a crevasse. After my initial incident I knew that I had to think more holistically about the approach to being safe, still having fun when I could have fun.

Everybody's trip is different because everybody has a different tolerance for how much risk they want to take on.

The expert is always thinking about the what ifs? What if something happens?

End of the Expert's Reflections

What are the five key points you developed?

Key Points Generated by ChatGPT-4

Note: OpenAI has attached the following to its webpage "ChatGPT can make mistakes. Check important info." Do you agree with what has been summarized?

Respect Terrain Warnings and Stability Assessments:

Adhere strictly to the guidelines given by those with more experience and avoid slopes that have been deemed unsafe, even if they appear only slightly steeper or different from approved routes.

Understand Snowpack Layers and Instability:

Recognize the dangers posed by layers of low-density snow on top of weak layers like buried surface hoar. This setup is a classic trigger for avalanches, especially after recent storms.

Minimize Exposure and Make Safety a Priority:

Always be cautious and minimize your exposure on suspect slopes. Encourage clients to follow your path only after you've confirmed stability and ensure they keep a safe distance.

Use Proper Avalanche Mitigation Techniques:

Employ techniques such as ski cutting to test slope stability before allowing others to follow. Ensure these cuts are long enough to effectively release any unstable snow.

Trust Your Instincts and Be Prepared to Adapt:

Pay attention to gut feelings and environmental cues. If something feels off, stop and reassess the situation, even if it means turning back or taking a less exciting route.

The Balance – Balancing Risk and Adrenaline in Unpredictable Conditions

Read the following scenario developed from an interview with an expert and stop at the decision point question as indicated by the statement...

"Write down your cues, goals, and what are you thinking/doing."

The following is very important and is how you will learn using this method.

Put yourself in the place of the expert and write down what you would be thinking and or doing if you were in that situation. **If you don't take the time to do this... you won't learn.**

Note that the information in the scenario might be incomplete, much the same as it would be in the real world.

<u>Do not skip ahead</u>. Reading ahead to see what the expert has done before you have put your thoughts down, will negate the value of this exercise.

After you have put your thoughts on paper refer to the next page "Thoughts of the Expert...". Have you differed or missed something? Think about that.

Continue reading the scenario sections, writing down your thoughts, and reading those of the expert until you come to the end. Reflect about the situation. In the same position, would you make the same decisions? What would be the outcome of those decisions?

Read the Expert's reflections to gain context and deeper understanding.

During your review of the expert's scenario and their thoughts, write down 5 key points. Compare your 5 to those developed by ChatGPT-4.

If you have any questions or comments, please reach out to
helicourse@gmail.com

The Balance 1

You are hired to be avalanche safety for an extreme skiing event in SE Alaska. Based out of a lodge, there are 100 adrenaline charged athletes chomping at the bit, ready to go. It has been snowing for days and you haven't been able to fly out to check the terrain or do any control work. At last, the storm breaks overnight and you wake up early to crip, cold, and clear blue sky. Game on.

The run has been chosen by the organizers and your job is to make sure it is safe for the skiers. This area is renowned for having deep powder snow that is very stable, generally only sluffing and sliding immediately after a snowfall. This allows for powder skiing in steep terrain. For various reasons you are unable to obtain or to use explosives to stabilize the slope. The helicopter takes you to the top of the mountain with three other avalanche techs.

After landing on the ridge above the run, you walk out on your skis towards the top of the venue with your partner spotting you, slowly poking your way out onto the slope until you feel the snow get a little bit stiffer under your feet. You take one more step and then stomp on the snow, triggering the slope right under your skis into a size 2 slab avalanche that runs down the whole venue.

(1). Write down your cues, goals, and what are you thinking/doing.

Do not skip ahead

Thoughts and Actions of the Expert 1

I had this feeling, like I could feel the slab getting progressively stiffer under my feet with each step, so after I had stomped and triggered the avalanche, I shuffled back to the ridge and said "OK, we're done. We're not doing it. We can't put people on this slope today and we have no explosives to remove the hazard."

So we got in the helicopter, lifted off and as we're turning to go back I realized, "Oh my God, I'm going to have to land back at the lodge on a perfect blue sky day with all these excited, pent-up skiers and tell them it is not happening."

I thought "There has to be a better way. I have to get this thing going, that's my job. That's what I was hired to do." So we turned the machine around, went back to the landing, and this time we planned out a way to control the venue.

There were four of us and because two of us were alpine climbers and we were in Alaska, we'd brought a climbing rack and a two ropes with us. We broke into two groups of two and we belayed our way down the venue, ski cutting the slope. Just like climbing up, putting in anchors and belaying a rope length, we did the same descending. Put in anchors, belay the guy down, ski cut the avalanche on an angle from the belay.

The lowered guy would then build an anchor and bring his partner down. We just worked our way down the whole thing in what looked like two parallel passes of zig zag ski cuts. We ski cut all the fresh avalanches off the face. Not all of them were that large but we cleaned the face off. Took us about an hour and a half to do that.

We held the competition that afternoon but by the time we ran it, the instability was gone. Fast. It had healed itself, as was typical for the area. I think that if we had not actually done all that ski cutting, I probably could have just run the event in the afternoon anyway.

But I didn't have the confidence for that. I mean, I wasn't going to get the whole thing going just using my feelings that it's probably going to be fine to ski in an hour. Perhaps if I was a local and more familiar with the snowpack I would have that confidence, but not this time.

"The problem with emotion and passion is they tend to be black or white, with no room for the nuance required to understand most topics. You can get a false sense of confidence, one that's disguised as absolute truth." Morgan Housel

The Balance 2

You are called back the next year to run avalanche safety for another extreme skiing contest out of a different part of SE Alaska. This is a much larger event with dozens of athletes, organizers, safety staff and media involved.

You have one week to prepare for the event and are given a partner, a truck, a magazine full of explosives, and a helicopter. You need to prepare three venues that meet specific criteria. The competition is starting on Friday with the athletes showing up Wednesday.

The organizers really want to hold the event on a specific run located on the east side of the range, and not in the usual location on the west side that they have used in other years. Every year they want to make the event more exciting than the last, and they've made it very clear that this year, they don't want to compete on last year's run - they want to up the game.

So you spend the week with your partner, who is a local guide, scoping venues, doing snow safety, lots of skiing, lots of inspecting and you focus most of your energy on the east side of the range where they really want to ski.

It has been a really tricky year as there was a deeply buried weakness in the snowpack, which was different than usual. Your initial investigations are showing a well-established layer of facets near the bottom of the snowpack, which is very concerning. This part of Alaska is coastal and known for its snow stability; it snows a lot here and the new snow generally stabilizes quickly, which allows for steep alpine powder skiing. But this year's proposed venue is further inland where, like any mountain range, the snowpack becomes shallower and the temperatures are colder. A culture of information sharing does not yet exist here, and so any information regarding snow safety from the established heliski operations is minimal.

You have received the odd report of a deep avalanche but the other operators are out skiing steep terrain like they normally do, very similar to your proposed venues, and reporting excellent conditions.

(2). Write down your cues, goals, and what are you thinking/doing.

Do not skip ahead

Thoughts and Actions of the Expert 2

I had done lots of deep digging down to the base of the snowpack and found this weakness which is not common in Alaska. That layer was not something that often happened there or that I thought I was going to find. I was surprised because I had expected to find a deep, solid snowpack like you might find at Whistler and I did not discover that.

The occasional report of a deep avalanche was really unnerving me because those kind of avalanches are somewhat unpredictable and difficult to control conventionally with explosives. So this information is kind of happening in the background, and I'm becoming uncomfortable with our east side venue but the wheels of the event are in motion. The Discovery Channel was there to air the event, and there's over a hundred people involved with the entire event and a lot of expectation and building excitement. We had done avalanche control with explosives, ski cutting and we're getting ready to go open the event on the east side venue; the ball was definitely rolling.

Meanwhile I was becoming more and more worried about the deep weakness in the snowpack, but few others seemed concerned, so I was trying to ignore my feelings. Normally in this Alaskan snowpack your concern is the surface layers and you don't have to worry about deep stuff. So this was how I was approaching it, right or wrong. I got the impression that the locals felt the same way, judging by how they were skiing everything, and so I was taking my cues from them; I was I was kind of forcing myself to adapt to what is normal locally.

Still, I kept asking questions about the seasonal snowpack and what's happening in the big picture here. One experienced local guide spoke to me at length about the wind effect, which to me means yesterday. Wind is a short-term effect on the surface and generally stabilizes quickly. I wanted to know about the deep layers in the snowpack and what kind of weaknesses they were tracking. I never really got any answers to those questions.

I'm sure they were getting nonevent feedback because not many deep avalanches were happening and business as usual was working. They were still skiing great terrain and everything was going well. Maybe that's part of expertise, being able to detect subtle clues and see through non-event feedback? But this is very hard to do and perhaps only obvious in hindsight.

I felt kind of alone with my concerns. I was holding on to this piece of information that was bothering me and I wanted to be able to talk about it, but I just felt like other people didn't really take it as seriously as me. It was a lonely feeling giving me a sick pit in the stomach.

The Balance 3

The day before the competition, on a heliski run immediately adjacent to the eastern venue, with the same aspect and elevation, a natural avalanche releases late in the day and obliterates a set of recent ski tracks. Nobody is involved in the avalanche. It released on bed surface of facets on glacier ice; a big, dirty slab on dark ice that ran far and took out an earlier set of ski tracks.

(3). Write down your cues, goals, and what are you thinking/doing.

<u>Do not skip ahead</u>

Thoughts and Actions of the Expert 3

We had already used explosives and done extensive ski cutting on the eastern venue. The run was prepped and ready for the competition, but when I got the information about the adjacent avalanche late in the day, it just made me sick to my stomach. Like, I'm about to put the event on and this happens right next door.

I thought "I can't put dozens of people on this slope. I just can't do it with that kind of instability in the snowpack. I don't care if nobody else understands that. I understand it. So we're calling it."

I consulted with my immediate partners and they felt the same, but it was me who had to talk to the organizers and call it off the night before. That cancellation was a high-pressure decision for me and I felt I was making it in the face of a lot of adversity with so many people who were going to be disappointed. But it was so obvious to me what had to be done.

Now we had to find another venue and we scrambled to get ready. We ran the even the next day on the western venue where they'd held it the year before and this worked well. For the other venues, we pivoted and went closer to the coast where the snowpack was deeper and where this instability didn't exist. We pulled off a successful competition on a couple of different venues, we met the goals, and it worked. It all worked.

Our eastern venue slope didn't ever slide. I mean, we basically abandoned it and I never went back to it.

End of Scenario

The Expert's Reflections ...

I probably went to Alaska with the perception of this magically stable snowpack. That was the reputation of the place, but I quickly figured out, "Wait a second here, it's not like that."

You just need a certain kind of snow, some temperature and moisture variables, and you're going to have instability. So I had to sort of chip through my perceptions of that snowpack and eventually learn what was actually going on. I think that's a bit of why I was not calling it off earlier, I had the feeling, "This is supposed to be really good here."

You start these kind of jobs by skiing lots of different kinds of terrain, trying to find different aspects, different elevations, using your probe for snow depth and then you dig. I started to notice a weakness down there and thought, "Who else is noticing this?" I just remember nobody really taking it that seriously.

I've made many decisions that I don't actually know whether I'm right or wrong. I will never know. I can close a slope and then have someone go, "Ah, nothing happened, you should have kept it open." But nothing happening is actually what we want. We don't want to close something and then have something happen. That confirms our decision of course but this rarely happens. Most of the time we get non-event feedback, it doesn't slide. Still, the right outcome is to close it, have nothing happen, nobody gets hurt, and reopen it, but that goes against the way many people see things.

All the time we make decisions and then nothing happens. That doesn't mean we made a bad decision. Lots of times it's a really good decision. I feel good about it and I can defend it, but I don't have proof that it was either the right or the wrong decision.

It's easy to think, "Oh that guy made a bad decision because nothing happened and we could have run the event there." But most decisions I make, nothing bad happens, that's the whole point of making the decision; so nothing happens. Here's the world's perfect scenario that never happens. Perhaps we close a road. The slope avalanches and it stops right at the edge of the highway, damages nothing, and then we open it again.

Let's talk about decision making on an avalanche path with a 50-year return. So that means it slides every 50 years, I might close it down once a winter and people have to evacuate. And then nothing happens. So they come back and well, that's just how it is.

It comes down once every 50 years, but I don't know what year that is and I don't know when that's going to be. So that means that when the hazard gets elevated, I'm going to close it and almost for sure nothing's going to happen, except every now and then. Once every 30 to 50 years, or twice, or two years in a row. Nobody knows.

Because we can't know that, our decision making has to be conservative in nature and we have to recognize most of the time nothing is going to happen. This is how you manage uncertainty. If you are a lay person looking at it, you're thinking, "Ah geez they have closed this place down and nothing happened. What a bunch of idiots." This is in fact the complete opposite of how I look at it.

Every situation is a little bit different. I mean, ideally you could use explosives and blow the hell out of the thing. That helps a lot with the confidence, but it's still not 100%. I mean, if I get a chance to use explosives I will. That's how we do it on the highway. We close it down, we pop it full of explosives and unless there is something really weird going on, we're going to open it back up again.

Explosives are helpful. Time is helpful, especially if you live in a dynamic snowpack such as Alaska or the West Coast. Most instabilities there are typically near the top of the snowpack and they're going to heal fast. You might get twice, three times as much snow there so it's unstable when just fallen, but it might settle quickly and the hazard could be gone in 24 hours.

Keeping people safe. That's actually my biggest goal, right? Safety. Well yes of course, but I want to run this event too. That's the whole reason why they brought me up there. But this creates serious motivational bias. Safety is not the first thing we think about, it's the second thing. The event is first, otherwise why would we even be out there doing this? Safety is a huge priority, but if it was the first priority then we would not even be there because extreme skiing is not safe.

People used to say to me "You are the safety guy." I would stop them and say, "No, I am the risk guy." Most people would roll their eyes, because they didn't understand what I was talking about. We don't do safety, we do risk management, which is about chance and the balancing probability and consequence.

Safety is about safety. It's about security, about not having anything happen. But the only way we can do that is by doing nothing. I consider probability and consequence to be as fundamental to our job as supply and demand is to an economist. They're huge. Everything, every single thing we do, is a balance of the probability and consequences. I think our motivations are primarily driven by the objective of what we set out to do, and then we try to manage risk around it by continuously evaluating probability and consequence and making adjustments. It's a constant, ongoing loop.

I find the hardest thing for us to do as rescuers is to make those decisions as to whether we're going to go in or not. The team is crucial for decision making because those types of decisions are not done on hard evidence, and because it's not an equation and there's no method that is going to tell us what's the right thing to do. We do it as a team and we work on consensus. Decisions always get better when a team is involved. It takes several people to be able to look at it from different perspectives and be able to see what the other person might have missed in order to get there. When I work in team decision making I say "argue like you are right and listen like you are wrong, and be prepared the change your perspective at any time."

Have I been lucky? OMG. Hundreds of times. I wouldn't be talking to you here if it wasn't for the role of luck in all this. It's crucial. I have so many friends who have passed and they necessarily didn't do anything different than me, they just (weren't lucky). I've had avalanches go over me. I've had rockfall whip past me. I've had incidents like falling off, you name it. I don't have as many of those anymore.

With regards to listening to my feelings, I don't increase the risk based on subjective feelings; the things we cannot explain. That's the wrong way to take on extra risk. If I'm trying to make decisions about whether or not I should keep going, or take more risk, I need evidence. I need a solid rational explanation. I will however reduce risk based on a feeling. Something might feel wrong, but I can't put my finger on it. I will happily retreat based on that.

I've learned over the years to listen to those feelings. I have been hit and had close calls countless times from not listening to those feelings. Most of those happened early in my career and that taught me that if you get a feeling like something is wrong here and you just can't say what it is, then get the hell out of there. I don't know what that is but something is giving you a message and you need to listen to it.

But if I get this feeling that says things are awesome but I can't explain it, that's not good enough for me to go forward. I need evidence or a rational explanation to increase the risk or to keep going. When I see others doing this, I like to ask for their rationale.

What an inexperienced person doesn't have is the ability to step out from the details in order to see the bigger picture; to see beyond what is right in front of them. They're not seeing all of it. I consider the ability to move from detailed assessment to big picture and then back to details a crucial marker of expertise. From big picture strategy to detailed tactics and then back again. You need to know where and when to do both of these. This only comes with experience, and this kind of experience generally begins by learning and mastering the details, followed by stepping back and seeing the big picture. There is no substitute of experience to acquire this kind of expertise.

It is kind of like the scale of a map. You can get right down into the 10 meter contours and you're looking at precisely every detail in the terrain. But you still have to be able to back out of those details, like to a map of British Columbia and see how it all fits in and how it fits together. I think that when you develop expertise, you can effortlessly move back and forth from both. You can get into the details and you can step into the big picture.

If you enjoy being with the people who are your mentors and they are getting something out of it, then it works. The people who are my most influential mentors are still important people to me to this day.

Sometimes things don't always have to be complicated. Sometimes it really is just a straightforward walk up the slope. People have a tendency to overcomplicate things when they lack the experience.

Everybody sees the world a little bit differently. Everybody has a little bit of difference in their risk tolerance.

End of the Expert's Reflections

What are the five key points you developed?

Key Points Generated by ChatGPT-4

Note: OpenAI has attached the following to its webpage "ChatGPT can make mistakes. Check important info." Do you agree with what has been summarized?

Risk and Safety:

Risk is different from safety. To move forward is to take a risk therefore probability and consequence must be considered.

Do not increase risk based on feelings but on evidence. However it is perfectly valid to reduce risk without being able to explain why.

Adaptation and Problem-Solving:

In the absence of explosives, develop alternative methods to stabilize the slope. For example, use climbing techniques like belaying and ski cutting to manage avalanche risk.

Collaborate with team members to methodically ski cut the slope, ensuring thorough control and minimizing hazards.

Communication and Stakeholder Management:

Clearly communicate decisions and the reasons behind them to all stakeholders, including event organizers and participants, even if it involves canceling or delaying the event.

Be prepared to handle disappointment and pressure from stakeholders who may not fully understand the safety implications.

Environmental and Snowpack Analysis:

Conduct thorough snowpack assessments, paying attention to deep layers and potential weaknesses, especially in unfamiliar areas where local knowledge might be lacking.

Stay informed about recent avalanche activity in the area and adjust plans accordingly based on the latest information and observations.

Risk Management and Decision-Making Under Uncertainty:

When dealing with high uncertainty, emphasize conservative decision-making. Taking on additional risk requires evidence and solid rationale. If you can't explain your rationale, then its not good enough.

Trust your experience and intuition when assessing risks, but ensure that decisions are backed by solid evidence and rational explanations whenever possible.

Balance the goals of safety and event success, always prioritizing the safety of participants.

Dragon Buttons - Navigating Uncertainty: Instinct, Terrain, Risk

Read the following scenario developed from an interview with an expert and stop at the decision point question as indicated by the statement...

"Write down your cues, goals, and what are you thinking/doing."

The following is very important and is how you will learn using this method.

Put yourself in the place of the expert and write down what you would be thinking and or doing if you were in that situation. **If you don't take the time to do this... you won't learn.**

Note that the information in the scenario might be incomplete, much the same as it would be in the real world.

<u>Do not skip ahead</u>. Reading ahead to see what the expert has done before you have put your thoughts down, will negate the value of this exercise.

After you have put your thoughts on paper refer to the next page "Thoughts of the Expert...". Have you differed or missed something? Think about that.

Continue reading the scenario sections, writing down your thoughts, and reading those of the expert until you come to the end. Reflect about the situation. In the same position, would you make the same decisions? What would be the outcome of those decisions?

Read the Expert's reflections to gain context and deeper understanding.

During your review of the expert's scenario and their thoughts, write down 5 key points. Compare your 5 to those developed by ChatGPT-4.

If you have any questions or comments, please reach out to
<u>helicourse@gmail.com</u>

Dragon Buttons 1

You are guiding a heliski group in the Coast Mountains. You have a really bad deep persistent weak layer (DPWL) and the other operations around you are having problems with it too. You are having difficulty getting an understanding of the hazard in the snowpack.

On this particular alpine run, there is a very specific hump like feature running all the way down that makes it easy to say to the group "You can't go to the right of this hump. It is a cross loaded slope." The wind had been depositing snow on the right side of the hump but on the left, it is reasonably scoured and stable. You pick the line that is the very edge of the stable snow trying to give the guests as much room to ski on the left side. The guests, a bit crowded together, follow instructions and ski to your left to stay on the correct side of the hump.

You are most of the way down to the pickup when the helicopter pilot radios "Avalanche, avalanche, avalanche." He lifts the machine up and out of the way as the slide covers the pad underneath him. You look back to see that everyone is safe because they have stayed to your left and you can't see the avalanche or its trigger.

(1). Write down your cues, goals, and what are you thinking/doing.

<u>Do not skip ahead</u>

Thoughts and Actions of the Expert 1

When I looked back carefully and then flew back up the line, I saw that one of my guests had done figure 8's on my track. His turn on the outside right just over the edge of the hump had triggered the avalanche. I was cutting the line way too fine, I should never have been there. It wasn't my guest's fault. There wasn't enough room to the left for fresh tracks for everyone, so in order to get some good turns he was behind me and just a little bit right on one turn as he was figure eight-ing my tracks. That's what triggered the DPWL and caused the avalanche.

Terrain selection becomes the next piece of the intuitive understanding of how not to trigger the deep instability.

If you look at the side of a mountain, it's a side of a mountain, but if you look at the line where you are going to ski down, it is only a metre wide, so there's a lot of choice of where you could go, even within that whole side of the mountain.

A guide might naturally be able to ski down and pick the right places to ski, but you put five people behind the guide and they may not.

Now put six groups on that run and you're going to ski it three times, the likelihood of finding that button gets higher. The button I refer to is the point where you can trigger the deep instability. The guide will ski in the right place but maybe the guests won't because they simply don't know. In avalanches that occur with guided groups, it's almost always the guest that sets it off because most of the time the guide is skiing in good terrain

The likelihood of finding the button increases as you ski more of the run.

There's a concept of over skiing a run. Ski the first line and it's the safest line down the run, the next guide skis the next safest line but theoretically the more you spread out and the more you ski that line, the more you vary from the first line that you skied, which is naturally the safest. Unsurprisingly it becomes less safe the further you get away from the original line.

Don't park your helicopter where it can get hit by an avalanche. Pilots are excellent at flying but may not have your avalanche safety sense.

Benford's Law of Controversy states that passion is inversely proportional to the amount of real information available.

Dragon Buttons 2

You are now the guide in charge of a Coastal heliski operation. It has been a relatively normal winter but there is a deep persistent weak layer (DPWL) buried in the snowpack. You have been discussing the run list with the other guides and have been marking certain runs red (no one is allowed to ski it) because you are worried about triggering the DPWL whereas the rest of the crew support marking it green for open.

You leave for your week of time off and upon your return you find the crew had unanimously made the runs you were concerned about green. In three instances, the day after they skied each of them, there was a release on the run that buried their ski tracks.

(2). Write down your cues, goals, and what are you thinking/doing.

<u>Do not skip ahead</u>

Thoughts and Actions of the Expert 2

I was keeping it red based on my intuitive knowledge. I had probably been through five or six of these deep unstable snow packs by that time, knowing that the way to treat them is basically to just stay away.

If you don't know, you don't go.

It's difficult for a skier to trigger the DPWL but the instability is still there. If you find the right button to push, the weakness pops and it usually propagates big and making large destructive avalanches. Terrain selection becomes the next piece of that intuitive understanding of not triggering the deep instability

The tricky part is that one, it's really hard to trigger unless you find the right button to push and then it's actually quite easy and two, the negative feedback loop that you get is really significant. You're constantly expanding into bigger, more aggressive terrain as you move through your guiding program naturally over the weeks. And nothing happens. Nothing happens. Nothing happens. And then, oh shit, the sleepy dragon wakes up. Yeah, and then it's usually big and catastrophic.

Because it's deep, the triggers for the DPWL are often shallower points. It's really difficult for a skier to trigger something a meter or more down as you just don't have enough pressure. A group of skiers standing in one spot might be able to create enough pressure to cause a fracture at that point, but typically what happens in ski groups is they find a shallow place that the wind has been on, where it's been scoured a little bit. So that deep instability that is a meter plus down everywhere else is only 50 centimeters down there. The skiers can trigger it causing it to propagate into the deep part of the snow pack, and then the whole thing runs.

Features that are conducive to triggering a deep instability are reasonably innocuous, but when all combined together they make a run, in my opinion, more risky or too risky compared to the other runs that we were skiing. That means we could ski a run and yet close a similar one right beside it.

These buttons are sometimes indicated by uneven snow distribution. You are looking for triggers on slopes that have shallow points, have rocks, have inconsistent snow cover over the run, convexities versus concavities, variable snow distribution, how the wind moves across the slope, where the snow is deposited and scoured, and evidence of pepper (small little rock outcrops that signify shallower snowpack areas).

Sometimes the snowpack builds up in such a way where the upper layers are reasonably stable over that DPWL. This builds up into a much deeper, buried instability and that's when at a certain point the snowpack basically starts to bridge over the weakness. We call it bridging, but it's a terrible word because it implies stability. At what point does the bridge break?

How do you know when the sleeping dragon, the DPWL is safe? You don't. It will likely never be. Bridging is a double edged sword. Bridging protects that weakness when the snowpack gets deep enough and or strong enough. You could take it to the degree where you could drive a tank over it, and because snowpack is so strong, it won't trigger that deep instability.

Now find a spot where it's shallow and it's not well bridged, not only will the tank trigger it but a skier will trigger it too. So bridging means the snowpack above the weaknesses is strong, but it also means that once triggered it'll propagate over great areas, like kilometres.

And so I was making the runs that had a higher likelihood of finding that deep instability, due to a prevalence of trigger spots.

My impression of their thinking was the first time the tracks got buried was just to brush it off. The second time was coincidence but by the third time it was maybe I should think about this more. So they were learning, but they weren't there yet. It took time, it took the positive feedback loop to kind of set in to finally change and overwhelm the negative feedback.

Most of them had never experienced that kind of persistent instability and because they had never experienced it, there was there was nothing in their toolbox to be able to deal with it. It wasn't even on their radar.

I would suggest that when I was making the runs red I probably wasn't explaining things well enough to paint the picture. Probably I was just doing it intuitively, "No I'm not going there. So we're not going there."

So maybe the mentorship wasn't flowing properly.

It's not a good learning environment, you know, to just have an old guy telling you the way it is, mostly because a lot of us old guys don't even really understand what it is we know or how to communicate it.

End of Scenario

The Expert's Reflections ...

There have been many instances where lesser experienced people have done things and I've taken them aside and said, "Hey, you know, that probably wasn't the greatest thing to do today." And their response is "Well, nothing happened, so fuck off."

It's extremely difficult to explain to someone the reasoning for doing or not doing something when the outcome was satisfactory or safe.

I explain to them that yeah, you could do that 100 times, but when will it be that one time that will get you? You don't know if it will be the first time or the hundredth time that you do it. It's just not the right thing to do given the conditions that we have. And so the idea of positive outcomes to potentially dangerous scenarios is something we as guides fight all the time. This is the negative (or nonevent) feedback loop.

There is a really big difference between having instant feedback and knowing that what you did is wrong and doing something over and over and over without feedback. You can do something in ski guiding, do it wrong all your career and never know you're doing it wrong because you don't get spanked. Or you could do it wrong the first time and get spanked. This is referred to as a wicked learning environment where there is no negative feedback to guide your decision making until it goes wrong.

I think a lot of inexperienced guides miss out on the idea that they don't know what they don't know. The negative feedback loop reinforces their decision making until they get to a point where either they have that mistake, or it happens to someone around them and they can learn from it.

We had one guide who would constantly go and take one step too far and get spanked. Luckily he was surviving them. I said "You can't keep doing this. You have to step back."

He replied 'Yeah, but if I step back, I'm going to be skiing the old boring runs just like you."

That's the point. By not stepping out too far you get to keep skiing and not get spanked, or worse. The personal pressure that guides put on themselves is very, very high and you combine that with the negative feedback loop where they seldom get feedback that says what they're doing is wrong and it lulls them into taking it a step out further every time. That negative feedback loop is the bane of a guides existence.

Unfortunately, a lot of that pressure is internal. Part of it is to provide good skiing to the customer and to be in a cool place that they'll really enjoy. And that that pressure is very strong, especially amongst younger guides.

At some point in time your gut feeling is actually a valuable decision-making tool, based on invaluable experience.

I can't ever think of an instance where I was using a gut feeling to drive me forward into more aggressive terrain. To me, gut feelings are what pulls you back, they put the brakes on. It is never "Oh, I've got feeling that this is going to be OK."

I think most guides would say to move forward, they need a concrete reason to believe as to why it's acceptable to do something. It could still be wrong, but they have to have a reason why they thought it was acceptable to support a gut feeling.

Mentorship comes from a vast skill set. I've seen that, I've done this, I've been through this. And that's not just me, that's any other, person who has a similar skill set or a similar amount of experience. They have probably done stupid shit, they've been involved in the stupid shit, they've seen stupid shit. They figured out how not to do it after time and it's unfortunate that it's the old close calls that really provide that learning opportunity. You have to learn from those because if you don't...

Unfortunately it is often you've learned a lesson through devastating consequences you have lived through, something really bad, or from someone else who has had something really bad happen to them.

Someone is considered an expert because of their decision making, experience, and skills. Real expertise is indicated by the following thought "I don't know if I know enough, and I don't know what I don't know." It is important to always be learning.

End of the Expert's Reflections

Editor's Note: The expert uses "negative feedback" which regulates a system (e.g. a thermostat) instead the more accurate "nonevent feedback" which describes a situation where doing the wrong thing still gives you the correct answer.

What are the five key points you developed?

235

Key Points Generated by ChatGPT-4

Note: OpenAI has attached the following to its webpage "ChatGPT can make mistakes. Check important info." Do you agree with what has been summarized?

Terrain Selection and Hazards:

Pay close attention to specific terrain features, like the hump mentioned in the scenario, that indicate areas of potential instability. Understanding and identifying cross-loaded slopes and wind-affected zones are critical to maintaining safety.

Group Management and Communication:

Ensure guests understand and adhere to instructions, especially in hazardous areas. Clear communication is vital to keep the group on the safest path and avoid triggering avalanches.

Understanding and Respecting DPWL:

Deep Persistent Weak Layers (DPWL) are challenging to predict and manage. Avoid skiing in areas with a high likelihood of triggering DPWL, even if the surface seems stable. Recognize that multiple runs and skier tracks increase the chance of triggering these layers.

Helicopter and Pickup Zone Safety:

Always choose safe locations for helicopter landing and pickup zones, considering avalanche risk. Ensure pilots understand and respect avalanche safety protocols.

Mentorship and Experience:

Value and seek out mentorship from more experienced guides. Learn from their insights and experiences, particularly regarding deep instabilities and the importance of conservative decision-making to avoid catastrophic events. Always be aware that intuition and gut feelings, backed by experience, are essential in making safe decisions.

Risk management is not equal to getting lazy

Sled Bowling – using terrain appropriately

Read the following scenario developed from an interview with an expert and stop at the decision point question as indicated by the statement...

"Write down your cues, goals, and what are you thinking/doing."

The following is very important and is how you will learn using this method.

Put yourself in the place of the expert and write down what you would be thinking and or doing if you were in that situation. **If you don't take the time to do this... you won't learn.**

Note that the information in the scenario might be incomplete, much the same as it would be in the real world.

<u>Do not skip ahead</u>. Reading ahead to see what the expert has done before you have put your thoughts down, will negate the value of this exercise.

After you have put your thoughts on paper refer to the next page "Thoughts of the Expert...". Have you differed or missed something? Think about that.

Continue reading the scenario sections, writing down your thoughts, and reading those of the expert until you come to the end. Reflect about the situation. In the same position, would you make the same decisions? What would be the outcome of those decisions?

Read the Expert's reflections to gain context and deeper understanding.

During your review of the expert's scenario and their thoughts, write down 5 key points. Compare your 5 to those developed by ChatGPT-4.

If you have any questions or comments, please reach out to
helicourse@gmail.com

Sled Bowling

You and your friend have been skiing for years and are experienced in traveling through avalanche terrain. Some acquaintances who are newish snowmobilers are keen to learn about avalanche safety from you and have asked for guidance. It is decided that the group will start with digging a snow profile in order to begin to understand layers and stability.

The six of you leave the Frisby Ridge parking lot outside of Revelstoke and sled up into the alpine. The ridge is heavily traveled, and it is quite a challenge to find a piece of untracked snow, so you drop down the east side of the ridge to the bottom of the big east facing bowl. It tends not to get sledders because it's a bit too steep.

You look at the bowl and think "Yeah, I would ski this. The hazard is low to moderate, there is no persistent weak layer, and there is nothing that I would trigger. Let's go into the bottom of this bowl and see if we can find a place that's undisturbed." The route follows the edge of the runout down into the bowl. You lead the group down and poke around the runout, finding a spot to teach profiles that is relatively undisturbed.

Your friend is uncomfortable with the location and doesn't want to be there.

(1). Write down your cues, goals, and what you are thinking/doing.

Do not skip ahead

Thoughts and Actions of the Expert

I was kind of like, what's the problem? I would ski this right now. Yes, we're at the base of the avalanche slope. But the hazard is low and the likelihood of triggering a size 3 and having it come to the bottom of the runout is really low.

But I agreed with my friend, and we moved around the corner into the non-threatened terrain, out of the runout zone. We found some undisturbed snow to begin digging profiles.

Later on I thought about that, because I'm usually a pretty conservative decision maker and here I was getting called on my decision saying I was being too aggressive. I was thinking, was I really being aggressive? I would ski this, it's good to go. I would totally ski this and feel comfortable having a helicopter pick us up at the bottom of the runout zone. I am confident in my snowpack assessment. Yes, the terrain is big. Yes, it's an avalanche slope. Yes, it has the potential to produce a size three or bigger avalanche that could run to this point. But then I had a shift in how I thought about the problem. I changed from applying a ski guiding lens to applying an avalanche educator's lens of teaching. The goal was to teach someone how to collect snowpack information. The goal was not skiing.

So here it is, a simple protocol, don't park your group in a run out zone when you're doing a stationary lesson. This is simply linking the educational objective with the use of terrain. We did not need to park at the bottom of the big avalanche slope to be able to dig in the snow. When you're working as an avalanche instructor, choose terrain that's appropriate to the learning objective.

You also have to be thinking, "How much risk do I need?" So when dealing with the risk environment, how much do I need to achieve my objective? I think of this scenario, where there is a piece of terrain that is capable of producing large avalanches. The hazard is low. Should we go there? The answer is if your goal is to go skiing or sledding, then yeah, absolutely. But if your goal is to do a rescue practice or to dig a profile, you don't need to be there. Why expose your group? **End of Scenario**

The Expert's Reflections ...

At the time I was annoyed. What do you mean you don't want to dig profiles here? It's totally fine. But I get it now. I was working with a peer, whom I respected highly. So when they suggested a more conservative course of action, it was a good idea to listen. I see it as being indefensible to say, "Well, no, we should stay here."

A way to think about hazard is exposure time in terrain. For example, the difference between skiing up a line and skiing down it. If you take 15 minutes to ski down a 1000 metre ridge your exposure time is less than if you spend an hour and a half skinning up. The hazard grows if you put a group of 44 heliskiers down that piece of terrain where each of them only skis it for 15 minutes but there's 44 tracks, so cumulatively your exposure is much higher and so is your potential for triggering a weak spot.

The force exerted on the snow in the ski touring up track will be a constant, similar to the static load, as opposed to skiing downhill where we apply dynamic forces. Think of pressuring a ski and then coming up in the air and dropping down into the next turn. Each time we drop down into that turn we're exerting a greater force.

I kind of think of it as if there's a landmine. When you're skiing downhill you're only maximizing your pressure 50% of the time. And the other 50% of the time you're unweighting whereas skinning the up track you are at a lesser but consistently even pressure the whole time.

It is different if we apply that lens to sledding. The uphill track has the same exposure as the downhill track - it takes the same amount of time. That thousand metre climb up might take 4 minutes up and another 4 minutes to come back down. Because of the larger footprint, the static load of the sled with the rider, even though heavier in combination than the skier, is only 1.3 times larger.

But the sled at full throttle in the uphill climb digs a deep trench and puts a greater load on the snowpack compared to sledding straight downhill. This is the opposite of a skier. The spinning track creates an additional force, so if you're spinning your track at 80 KMH, the three inch paddles are digging down into the snow. That rotational mass of the track spinning and digging puts the sled closer to a buried weak layer and amplifies the load. The amount of force is 5 to 10 times greater than what a skier would generate. So when we think of sleds going uphill, they are stressing the snowpack much more than a skier going up the same slope.

If you're sledding and you get caught in a slide, what should you do? We developed a process for that. If you're climbing up and you trigger something, then the best strategy is to point straight uphill, hit the throttle and try to climb out of the avalanche. Hopefully, you're not that far from the crown and you have a bit of momentum. Hitting the throttle might just pop you out the top.

If you're further down into the avalanche and are pointing downhill, you may be able to outrun it. The challenge is that although you have speed, momentum, and gravity on your side, you still have to control the sled. You could hit the stauchwall at the bottom of the slab which can be a metre deep. There are really good videos of guys hitting stauchwall and just ejecting. And then there's hitting the trees. How much control do you have? Sure, you can get the speed going, but do you have control? So, yes, there are people who have outrun avalanches, but generally, unless you're low in the track you're probably not going to outrun it. You're probably going to get caught up in it.

How do I think about terrain selection for sledding? I start by making that decision in the morning, where I'm applying the avalanche hazard to the terrain with my knowledge of what's going on in the snowpack and my understanding of the terrain so that I don't have to make an on slope decision in the moment.

Sledding does not use a run list like heliskiing. We use zones and describe open and closed terrain. For example we'll say, "Open today is all slopes below 30° up to the tree line.

Closed will be steeper than 35°, tree line and above." It helps us describe the terrain within a zone. It might be that "On Frisby that's what we'll do but if we go over to Boulder then maybe we can go up to 35° on terrain that has been more modified due to extensive slope use."

But what to do when the analysis says it's all good and the intuition says no, or vice versa? We need to listen to both voices. We will have done an in depth analysis looking at snow pack structure and distribution, all of the information from our nearest neighbors. It may lead to a decision that a particular slope is safe to use. It's good to go. But if we get to that slope and think, "I don't like this." Now we're going to think about why? What's going on? What's different? What did I miss in my analysis?

We run into those dilemmas of which way should I go, which course of action is appropriate? If we have a default of taking the conservative choice, then we live to ski another day. We live to ride another day. If we choose the conservative option and we were wrong, that is OK. It's OK to be wrong, because we got home. However if you choose the more aggressive line and you're wrong and people die, that's not OK,

End of the Expert's Reflections

What five key points have you developed?

Key Points Generated by ChatGPT-4

Note: OpenAI has attached the following to its webpage

"ChatGPT can make mistakes. Check important info."

Do you agree with what has been summarized?

Terrain Choice for Teaching:

Choose terrain appropriate to the learning objective. Avoid exposing the group to unnecessary avalanche risk during stationary activities like digging snow profiles.

Hazard Assessment and Intuition:

Even with thorough analysis showing low hazard, listen to your intuition and peers when they express concern. It's crucial to err on the side of caution, especially when others feel uncomfortable.

Risk Exposure Time:

Understand the impact of exposure time. Whether skiing, skinning, or snowmobiling, the longer you spend in hazardous terrain, the greater the risk of triggering an avalanche. For snowmobiling, especially during uphill climbs, the added load on the snowpack is significant.

Impact:

Snowmobiles apply much more stress on the snowpack compared to skiers, especially when climbing. The dynamic forces exerted by spinning tracks increase the risk of triggering a buried weak layer.

Emergency Response During a Slide:

In case a snowmobile triggers an avalanche, the best strategy is to either accelerate uphill or, if possible, outrun the slide downhill. However, control can be difficult, and the decision should be made based on your position relative to the slide.

"It is much more difficult to acknowledge that something is excellent and then to ask for change because although it is excellent, it is not enough." Edward De Bono

Did you See That? - Unexplainable evidence of instability

Read the following scenario developed from an interview with an expert and stop at the decision point question as indicated by the statement...

"Write down your cues, goals, and what are you thinking/doing."

The following is very important and is how you will learn using this method.

Put yourself in the place of the expert and write down what you would be thinking and or doing if you were in that situation. **If you don't take the time to do this... you won't learn.**

Note that the information in the scenario might be incomplete, much the same as it would be in the real world.

Do not skip ahead. Reading ahead to see what the expert has done before you have put your thoughts down, will negate the value of this exercise.

After you have put your thoughts on paper refer to the next page "Thoughts of the Expert...". Have you differed or missed something? Think about that.

Continue reading the scenario sections, writing down your thoughts, and reading those of the expert until you come to the end. Reflect about the situation. In the same position, would you make the same decisions? What would be the outcome of those decisions?

Read the Expert's reflections to gain context and deeper understanding.

During your review of the expert's scenario and their thoughts, write down 5 key points. Compare your 5 to those developed by ChatGPT-4.

If you have any questions or comments, please reach out to

helicourse@gmail.com

Did You See That?

You are working in SE BC as a heliski guide. It is early March and the day is shaping up to be fantastic with low hazard, no significant weak layers in the snow pack, and blue sky flying weather. The decision is made to make a grand tour of the big glaciers and steep trees at the back of the tenure.

You lift off from the lodge as the first of 4 ski groups and fly west for five minutes. Everything is looking good and as expected there is no new snow or wind effect, no new avalanche activity, and the temperature cools as you climb.

As you fly around the corner of a valley enroute to the big terrain you see a NE facing high elevation, moderate angle glacier with a size 3 avalanche, 3 to 4 metres thick, down to the ice. The crown is crisp, indicating that it has released within the last 12 hours.

(1). Write down your cues, goals, and what are you thinking/doing.

<u>Do not skip ahead</u>

Thoughts and Actions of the Expert

We all went out in the morning confident that we knew exactly what was going on and then suddenly our world view changed. We had this single piece of overwhelming evidence that I felt we couldn't ignore. It was just such a big, obviously fresh avalanche. The fracture line was crisp and it was on moderate planar terrain, not a steep or complex slope. It really shattered my confidence and threw so much uncertainty into our avalanche forecast and our plan for the day.

I was the first guide to see it so my reaction was to call the lodge, explain what I saw and say that we are changing plans and we are now going to ski low angle terrain for the day until we figure out what is going on. From the other guides who had not seen the avalanche yet there was a bit of resistance and lots of questions about the weather, the angle and aspect and elevation and all those quite normally relevant questions. All that resistance to a change of plans disappeared as the other guides flew over it and then understood the magnitude of the problem. I think everybody calmed down and we had ourselves a beautiful day. We basically agreed we were all very uncertain about what factors led to this avalanche and that we would just get through this day safely and really focus on it in the evening.

In conversation with other operations in the area that evening there was disbelief as there had been no other avalanche activity, anywhere. We did some digging and eventually got ahold of data from a USGS seismology centre in Golden, Colorado that showed there had been an earthquake in our area and we then had some confidence that an earthquake was what had triggered this unusual avalanche.

The Expert's Reflections ...

None of the other operators we spoke to that evening had seen any other avalanche activity. A couple of people were of the mindset that "Well, you know, shit happens. It doesn't change our hazard forecast." Shit that big doesn't just happen. In hindsight they were somewhat correct, it would have been OK to ski the original plan but it would be very foolish to ignore that piece of evidence.

The next day we were again comfortable to go back out and use the terrain as we had previously planned as we had restored our confidence and could believe that this was a onetime unusual occurrence.

What makes for good decisions? Fundamentally, I think part of making good decisions and addressing uncertainties is maintaining an open conversation from the start of your season or your trip and on the tailgate and throughout the day. Discussing things like "what could be different from our forecast", "what would make us turn around", "do we have a plan B", "is everybody aware of and comfortable with the plan?"

Being organized leads to better decisions. The more organized you are, the more time you have to think. If you have that person in your group in the parking lot who's got one ski boot on, eating a sandwich, and trying to find batteries for their transceiver, well, they are not really helping with the decision-making.

In a guided ski touring situation or generally being with others, it helps to make sure everyone is aware of the current conditions. These are our concerns. This is what's going on with the snowpack right now. This is this ski quality. It's good to try and educate everyone as to what we know and what we may not know.

You know when I first started ski guiding, avalanche awareness was generally very limited amongst the skiing population. That has changed dramatically over the years and now I find people are way better educated in Canada, certainly with Avalanche Canada, the

AST courses and the generally more easily available information. Even the ski movies are more open about avalanche problems. It seems to be a lot easier now to deal with people.

It's important to maintain that dialogue with whomever you travel in avalanche terrain with. I recommend if someone is going to do an AST, do it with the people you ski with, so you all have the same tool kit and the same language. There are many AST instructors, so there can be a lot of variation but that's not a problem if everybody takes the same course. You get a foundation to work with and then you just keep that conversation going from there.

Even if you just think you're nerding out it's good to be accumulating information and getting the picture in your head. But sometimes there is no information. I was ski touring in Albania and Kosovo last winter and you have nothing there related to avalanche conditions like a CAA bulletin. You can dig around and look at weather records but really, you've just come into it with your eyes wide open. In that case you're going to start with the simple terrain and then possibly creep out from there as your observations start to give you a better picture of what's going on.

The idea is to embrace the uncertainty. If something doesn't make sense, don't ignore it. Try to figure out what it is but mainly be willing to change your plans. Address the uncertainty. Some examples of events that could generate uncertainty would be the forecast was 20 cm new snow but you get 50 cm, or you see a big avalanche, or it is way warmer than expected. If you see any of these changes, recognize it and be able to reel in your plans.

Keep your mind and your eyes wide open. I'm always more conservative in flat light because you just lose terrain and snowpack clues. Good visibility allows us to really evaluate terrain and see clues like cornice falls, wind affect, or avalanche activity but sometimes it is the smaller dangers you need to see such as skiing hazards. One foggy day in Japan I was skiing down a valley poking around in the very flat light. I look ahead and think that the fog is really "boiling up" there. I stop and notice a tiny little skull and crossbones sign sticking out of the snow. We slide forward a bit and there is a deep depression about 20 m round full of boiling mud that you have to ski around. "Death on a stick" so to speak :)

Decision making in the mountains really reminds me of an old flying expression – "I'd rather be down here wishing I was up there, than be up there wishing I was down here."

Moving through avalanche terrain is an art and I like to stress the idea to never be ashamed to turn down your ambitions or just turn around if conditions and the terrain don't feel right.

End of the Expert's Reflections

What five key points have you developed?

Key Points Generated by ChatGPT-4

Note: OpenAI has attached the following to its webpage
"ChatGPT can make mistakes. Check important info."
Do you agree with what has been summarized?

Uncertainty and Evidence-Based Decisions:

Even when conditions seem stable, a single piece of significant evidence, like a fresh size 3 avalanche, can shatter confidence. Never ignore such evidence, even if it conflicts with prior stability assessments.

Terrain Selection for Safety:

When confronted with unexpected avalanche activity, it is crucial to adjust plans. In this scenario, transitioning to lower angle terrain (Plan D) was a cautious and effective response to uncertainty in the snowpack.

Communication and Convincing Others:

Sometimes it's challenging to convince others to change plans based on one observation. However, once the other guides witnessed the avalanche, they understood the magnitude of the situation and made more conservative decisions.

Unexpected Triggers – Earthquake:

The avalanche was caused by an earthquake, highlighting that avalanches can be triggered by factors beyond typical weather-related events. Always consider broader environmental factors, such as seismic activity.

Adapting and Learning from Experience:

Even though no other avalanche activity was observed, the decision to proceed cautiously in uncertain conditions was validated by the rare earthquake trigger. This highlights the importance of adjusting to changing conditions and learning from past experiences for better decision-making.

When things are unusual, unusual things happen.

A calm mind isn't the absence of conflict or stress, but the ability to cope with it.

Tip Toes – unprecedented conditions and influence

Read the following scenario developed from an interview with an expert and stop at the decision point question as indicated by the statement...

"Write down your cues, goals, and what are you thinking/doing."

The following is very important and is how you will learn using this method.

Put yourself in the place of the expert and write down what you would be thinking and or doing if you were in that situation. **If you don't take the time to do this... you won't learn.**

Note that the information in the scenario might be incomplete, much the same as it would be in the real world.

<u>Do not skip ahead</u>. Reading ahead to see what the expert has done before you have put your thoughts down, will negate the value of this exercise.

After you have put your thoughts on paper refer to the next page

"Thoughts of the Expert...". Have you differed or missed something? Think about that.

Continue reading the scenario sections, writing down your thoughts, and reading those of the expert until you come to the end. Reflect about the situation. In the same position, would you make the same decisions? What would be the outcome of those decisions?

Read the Expert's Reflections to gain context and deeper understanding.

As you read the expert's scenario and their thoughts, write down 5 key points. Compare your 5 to those developed by ChatGPT-4.

If you have any questions or comments, please reach out to
helicourse@gmail.com

Tip Toes 1

You have been working in avalanche control for ten years at a ski resort and have just been hired to work as an avalanche technician for an highways avalanche program. It is early December and the information from the areas around your operation is that the snowpack is unstable and other operations are starting to see more frequent avalanche activity as well as larger natural avalanche occurring.

There is a weak lower snowpack with cold shallow snow. The InfoEx has also been reporting a significant uptick in avalanche activity and size, failing in this weak and shallow snowpack layer with some releasing to ground. This type of instability is not common in this area.

With the supervisor on days off, you suggest that we should consider a highway closure and conduct avalanche control with a helicopter (helicopter bombing) on the avalanche paths above the highway. The other two more senior staff members dismiss your concerns and remind you that you are new to this operation and really don't have the experience to make that suggestion. Therefore no avalanche control was conducted that day.

The following day you are tasked to ski tour to the top of the mountain with another more senior staff member to dig a snow profile and gather more snowpack information. As you approach the upper starting zone of one of the avalanche paths above the highway, you are recalling the information you have gathered from the InfoEx and have concerns about the stability and weakness in the lower snowpack.

(1). Write down your cues, goals, and what are you thinking/doing.
<u>Do not skip ahead</u>

Thoughts and Actions of the Expert 1

Being told that you are new to the operation and didn't have the experience to make a judgement on what the current avalanche hazard was and when to conduct avalanche control my confidence. Maybe my place is not to make suggestions, but just follow direction. My concerns about the snowpack were dismissed so I thought to myself "Well, I am new to this operation and I am not completely familiar with the terrain, and maybe there are several things I don't really know. I will just follow their lead and do what I am told."

I should have showed them a little more the evidence and tried to convince them a little bit harder that we needed to go in and do some preventative actions, like heli bombing. If that hadn't of worked, I may have brought it up to the supervisor a little bit sooner by saying, "Hey, I have a concern. I think we have a bigger problem here than we're realizing. This is what we know, I would recommend we go and do this."

Tip Toes 2

You arrive at the start zone of the slide path and are told to traverse across it to a predetermined spot and dig a snow profile.

(2). Write down your cues, goals, and what are you thinking/doing.

<u>Do not skip ahead</u>

Thoughts and Actions of the Expert 2

We ski toured to the top of the avalanche start zone of this particular avalanche path. I started to poke out into the start zone. I am going really slowly and cautiously, tiptoeing as I start to look at how I am going to safely access the snow profile location. I was poking into the snowpack with my pole, which felt weak and "hollow". The snowpack also felt weak and hollow under my skis. I was nervous and I looked back a few times wondering to myself if trying to access the starting zone of the avalanche path to dig a snow profile was the right decision or not. I took one more half step and the entire slope failed to ground off the tips of my skis. The avalanche size was about a 2.5, and ran down towards the highway. The avalanche did impact the highway which was open at the time and it was fortunate that a vehicle was not struck.

If I would have been another metre into the starting zone I would have most certainly been caught in the avalanche, and the outcome would have been serious. The avalanche had released to ground and the ground cover was very rough and rocky.

I didn't know that the slope was going to release, I was just being very careful based on the information I had gathered over the last few days from the InfoEx and public bulletins. I knew the snowpack was poor and I was trying to find a reasonably safe spot to dig our profile and gather that critical snowpack information. If the avalanche had not released, I would have likely continued into the start zone to dig our snow profile.

I don't think I ever got to the point of thinking to myself "I am not going another step farther". I was being very, very careful in where I was going and moving slowing because of how the snowpack felt under my skis.

My "spider sense" was tingling and of course there is always uncertainty when assessing avalanche risks. It is a big piece of terrain and because of spatial variability, one is never sure exactly where the problem is within that terrain. We knew there was an instability out there but how sensitive is it, how widespread, how deep… ? These were all questions we were trying to answer and why we were out on our skis that day to gather critical information. We were trying to figure out the extent of the problem before we decided to close the road and conduct avalanche control. Closing the road has a big impact on all highway users so this decision is never taken lightly.

Although it was critical to gather snowpack data, and that was the main goal of the day, I should have chosen a different spot to gather that information, a less risky spot with minimal consequence if the slope did release. I should have pushed back a little bit and said to my co-worker "I don't feel comfortable in this location, let's try to find somewhere else to dig this profile and gather our information. A spot that is perhaps safer with less potential consequences.

Avalanche risk management for a highways operation is different from that of a ski hill or in the guiding industries. You can't just close the road at the end of the day, go home, and forget about it until the next morning. You are always "turned on". The highway is a 24/7 operation. In ski guiding, you have the ability to manage the risk through terrain selection, the highway can't be moved, so avoiding terrain is not an option.

So that part of the job was new to me, how risk management for highways differed from my experience working at a ski resort. At the ski resort, you are thinking about the vulnerability of a little kid getting caught even in a small avalanche, which could be catastrophic. When it comes to vehicles travelling through avalanche areas, the exposure is quite short with the speed of the vehicles and the vulnerability is different because a vehicle provides more protection than someone not in a vehicle. Due to the difference in vulnerability between ski resort guests and staff, and highway users, the risk tolerance is also different and that took some getting used to.

Perhaps someone who had less experience may not have been as careful in approaching the start zone in the way I did. If they were a little more aggressive, if they were just "head down" and were simply following direction, they may have just run right out there to start digging a snow profile.

The fundamental goal is for the safety of workers and the public.

Tip Toes 3

Several years have passed and you are now in charge of the program. A large rain event in November has turned the mountains blue with rock hard ice before the current December storm hits. There are two sections of the road that need avalanche control separated by 500 metres at the curve. You have closed the north section of the road to do avalanche control. The traffic is stopped, lining up at both edges of the north zone.

The avalanche control in the storm is successful, a little too successful as the slides are running big and fast on the November ice crust. Everything is coming down. The avalanche deposit removal in the north section is taking longer than expected and it won't be open for another two hours. The weather is getting worse. The traffic is continuing to back up beyond the curve and is now under the south slide path.

(3). Write down your cues, goals, and what are you thinking/doing.

<u>Do not skip ahead</u>

Thoughts and Actions of the Expert 3

I'm getting nervous that now we have vehicles stopped in the travel lanes. So, I got another traffic control person to halt traffic at the south end of the south section, which keeps any further traffic from stacking up at the curve. I then moved the backed up traffic forward into the curve using a parking lot and every available space to get them all out of the avalanche area.

Within 5 minutes of moving the traffic from the south side avalanche area, a large avalanche came down naturally and hit the road right where all of the traffic had been backed up. There was an initial report that a car had been hit which caused great concern and we initiated our avalanche rescue protocol. As it turned out, all of the vehicles had been moved to a safe location and there was no vehicle involvement. It was a very stressful incident.

The visibility was very poor, you could barely see 20 feet and you could hear avalanches running toward the highway, although all of the public and workers had been evacuated from the avalanche area. It was a scary event and could have turned out much worse if I had not recognized the increasing risk in both the traffic vulnerability and the avalanche hazard.

In the days after the incident, I reflected on the way we had managed our traffic when conducting avalanche control at the curve. The methodology of the traffic management had been well established for years and I was simply doing things the way they had been done for years. I felt that I needed to re-evaluate our traffic control strategy and needed to think about other options that might be inefficient but would avoid putting ourselves in an uncomfortable position. One of the goals of managing a highway or industrial avalanche risk management program is balancing the risk and operational goals. If we close too often we are not doing our job. If we stay open too long we are putting workers and / or public at risk. This incident changed the way we managed traffic and although closures are now a bit longer, the difference ended up being marginal but the increase in safety was significant.

I also realized that I had felt a lot of pressure to keep the road open as much as possible and be as efficient as possible when we did have to close the road. This introduced a bias into my decision making process. In the earlier years when I first started in this program, I often heard the senior staff talk about the pressure they felt to keep the highway open, and it was coming from upper management. That pressure was downloaded to the entire team and seemed to often be front and center in my mind when I was making decisions. I remember a meeting I had with my manger a few years later and I asked him about his expectation regarding closures and the pressure I felt to keep the highway open. My manager looked at me and said "Where did you get that idea, I have never told you that". He then said "I trust your decision making and you should do what you think it right".

It was like a lightbulb went off in my head. The pressure I had been putting on myself and the team to push it, to keep the road open was self-imposed. I had a perception that ended up not being correct. It felt like a weight had been taken off my shoulders.

Just because a process or method has been used for years by workers that have been in a program for a very long time, doesn't mean that improvements or changes shouldn't be made. Things change and evolve, such as traffic volumes and as a risk management professional, it is critical to be able to step back and objectively review process and procedures to see if there is room for improvement. I also remember hearing the senior staff talk about the potential, or lack of potential from certain avalanche paths. I would often hear "that path has never hit the road" or "that will never be a problem". That can also introduce bias. It was a good lesson in recognizing biases and trying not to have them drive your decision making.

End of Scenario

The Expert's Reflections ...

Working in an industrial or highways type avalanche risk management program does come with a significant amount of pressure to keep the goods and services moving and to minimize any impact to the public or the employer. There is a fine balance between closing too often and keeping the road open too long. I often tell managers that the avalanche program is not there to close the road. We are there to keep it open as long as possible, as long as we are managing the potential risk to a reasonable and acceptable level.

There is always uncertainty in avalanche forecasting, and as a forecaster you need to be aware of that and accept it. The more information you can gather, the less uncertainty you will have. If you are lacking in data or information, your uncertainty will increase. This should impact your decision making (more caution with increased uncertainty).

Even when you do err on the side of caution, you can still get surprised. Avalanche forecasting and risk management is not an exact science and you will not be 100% correct all the time. Therefore, you have processes in place to try and minimize any negative effects when you do get surprised (such as choosing a location to dig a snow profile).

There are always outside pressures, but the key is to try and not let them cloud your decision making process. Look for feedback, go test the snowpack, get out on your skis and feel the snow, identify areas where information is lacking and gather that information to reduce uncertainties.

Avalanche return periods are often expressed in "years of return", so for example a path might run full path only once in 3 years, or 10 years, or 30 years, or 100 years. The career of an avalanche technician is likely around 30 years, so there may be avalanche events that occur once, or even less than once, in a given career. It's important to keep that in mind when someone says "I've never seen that happen" or "that will never happen" that maybe it hasn't in their time in a program, but it doesn't mean it will never happen. Having "fresh eyes" on a problem is a good thing and should be embraced. It is important to recognize one's biases and good leaders are open to different points of view. I have learned not to dismiss others' opinions just because they are "new" to a program or have less experience.

For the new generations of avalanche workers, the training is getting better all the time as the industry innovates. Recognizing bias and human factors in decision making is more front and center in the training than it used to be, which helps people to be more grounded in their decision making.

When you are out in the mountains, always have your head up. Be observant and take in all of the information you possibly can (reduce uncertainty). Use that feedback to constantly calibrate your decision making. Maybe you need to change your objective based on the information you have gathered. Have options and don't get tunnel visioned into a goal or objective. Be flexible.

I don't ski tour with random people because I need to trust the people I am out with. Not only in skill sets, but also attitude. If everyone in your group is on the same page, has similar or aligned risk tolerances, and are ok with changing objectives based on group decisions, you won't be pushed to do something or go somewhere you are not comfortable with. I know of several accidents where poor group dynamics were a contributing factor.

Personally, I err on the side of caution when I am out ski touring and making decisions of where to ski. I wasn't always like that and certainly took more risks when I was younger but as I grew older and gained experience, I was more appreciative of the potential risk and what level of risk I was willing to accept.

End of the Expert's Reflections

What five key points have you developed?

Key Points Generated by ChatGPT-4

Note: OpenAI has attached the following to its webpage
"ChatGPT can make mistakes. Check important info."
Do you agree with what has been summarized?

Trust Your Instincts and Be Proactive:

If something feels wrong, like the snowpack structure being poor or the avalanche danger high, don't dismiss your concerns. Be proactive in proposing solutions, such as heli bombing, and don't let others' experience or authority discourage you from speaking up. Even if you're new, you bring a fresh perspective that could highlight risks others might overlook.

Know When to Push Back:

If the situation feels unsafe, it's important to speak up. Don't hesitate to voice concerns. In avalanche work, the consequences of small decisions can be life or death.

Risk Management is Constant and Dynamic:

Road avalanche control, unlike ski hill work, involves more continuous risk assessment. You have to constantly balance the need for safety (both of the workers and the public) with the pressure to keep the road open. Always be ready to adjust your actions based on the current situation and be prepared for unforeseen consequences.

Recognize the Limits of Experience:

Even seasoned experts can have blind spots, especially when it comes to decision-making in uncertain conditions. Recognize that just because a situation hasn't occurred in the past doesn't mean it can't happen. Trust your training and be open to new ideas, as conditions change, and new challenges can arise unexpectedly.

Continuous Learning and Reflection:

Avalanche work is an evolving field. Reflect on past incidents and be open to learning from them, including how different practices might improve safety. After an incident, take time to reflect and communicate your concerns to improve the team's decision-making and to prevent similar mistakes in the future.

AEP Participation Request

Experts were selected as suggested by other experts. The following email was then sent.

I am writing because it was suggested that you would be an important contributor to the Avalanche Expertise Project (AEP), joining the other experts who have already taken part.

The AEP is a resource designed to improve decision making skills related to avalanche safety. Your input can add valuable insights to the Project.

We will have a 60-90 minute conversation designed to explore your expert-level thinking, including the tacit or unexplainable aspects.

This interview involves you reflecting on a significant, non-routine situation where you were the primary decision-maker. We are interested in an event where something did or did not happen because of your decisions—an event where your expert decisions differed from what a novice might have made.

The interview aims to uncover the expertise that guided your actions. An anonymized scenario will be created from that experience.

Background:

I am a now retired 15,000 hour helicopter pilot putting my Masters of Adult Education to work. After ten years at Ski Lake Louise, flying heliskiing for a decade, and working avalanche control for 20 years, I have a peripheral knowledge of the avalanche world and great respect for those that work in it.

Expertise is fascinating no matter its area. My MEd thesis was about the innate crewing skills of some expert heliski guides and how they developed it. Common sense says that one gains wisdom from experience (10,000 hours?) but what if we could create methods that assist in the acquisition of wisdom? That assistance is my goal.

To this end I am using Cognitive Task Analysis (CTA) to gather the wisdom of avalanche experts and deliver it to others. One of the challenges of expertise is the curse of knowledge, the inability to understand just how complicated and nuanced one's thinking has become. This inability can interfere with the transfer of wisdom (up to 70%).

Laura Adams (2005) p. 234-5, recommended critical thinking training to enhance the development of critical thinking, situational awareness, and metacognition for those in the avalanche industry. CTA uses various strategies to capture both the explicit and implicit knowledge as well as the thinking that experts use to carry out complex tasks.

The CTA method involves the identification of an expert, who is then interviewed about an occasion where **their expertise made a difference in the outcome**. This recollection is then probed to capture context, cues, goals, expectations, and options. The recollection (or story) is then transcribed and both the interviewer and the expert review it to ensure it is accurate and complete.

For educational purposes the anonymized story is presented as a simulation, stopping at defined points to ask the learner a "What would you do now" question and getting them to reflect on the expert's actions. This technique enhances the development of critical thinking and the recognition of cues, assessments, potential errors, and options.

On a non-compensated basis, the Avalanche Expertise Project (AEP) will be a tool for the benefit of avalanche education in Canada. It will develop the critical thinking of those in the avalanche world as a work book, an online program, and/or delivered by an expert.

Reference: A Systems Approach to Human Factors and Expert Decision-Making Within Canadian Avalanche Phenomena, Laura Adams (2005). https://www.collectionscanada.gc.ca/obj/thesescanada/vol2/001/mr05127.pdf?is_thesis=1

Reference: Loopy Experts, Tony Walker (2020). https://static1.squarespace.com/static/601c4bb24dd3a619448cc865/t/635c3c8bd89bad67e74d804b/1666989196359/Loopy+Experts.pdf

Ethical Statement

This research is not carried out under the auspices of any educational institution, however the principles, practices, and procedures as outlined in the Tri-Council Policy Statement on Ethical Conduct for Research Involving Humans are followed.

Highlights include informed consent which can be withdrawn at any time, privacy through anonymization, review of to be published material, and no researcher conflicts of interest.

You may withdraw your consent, participation, and/or information from this project at any time.

OpenAI Participation

From the OpenAI website: "ChatGPT can make mistakes. Check important info."

Chat GPT 4 Cue for summarizing key points -
   "Using the viewpoint of an expert mountain guide, summarize the following scenario into 5 key points that would be valuable to the novice avalanche technician."

Chat GPT 4 cue for summarizing scenarios:
   "Develop a subtext for a table of contents encapsulating the subject of the scenario In 5 words."

1 – Rescue risks, judgment, and survival
2 – Pressure, judgment, risk, and consequences
3 – Heli-skiing uncertainty amidst unpredictable terrain.
4 – Balancing Avalanche Risk and Productivity
5 – Balancing Risk, Responsibility, and Thrill
6 - Confidence, Consequences, and Leadership Dynamics
7 - Strategic Avalanche Control Amid Pressure
8 - Avalauncher Decisions: Navigating Instability Risks.
9 - Avalanche Control: Assessing Hidden Triggers.
10 - Intuition, Terrain, Risk, Snowpack, Decisions
11 - Navigating Risk, Ego, and Responsibility.
12 - Risk Management, Leadership, Communication, Survival.
13 - Unexpected Risk, Intuition, Leadership Decisions.
14– Risk Awareness, Decision Bias, Consequence.
15 – Risk, Instincts, and survival in snow
16 – Balancing Risk and Adrenaline in Unpredictable Conditions
17 – Navigating Uncertainty: Instinct, Terrain, Risk
18– Avalanche Terrain, Decision-Making, Snowmobiling Safety.
19 – Unusual evidence, Uncertainty, Terrain Management
20 – Unprecedented Conditions and Influence

An Incomplete Cross Reference of scenarios

(Send suggestions to helicourse@gmail.com)

Heliski	2	3	5		10		13	15	17	19
Explosives		4		7 8					16	
Pressure		4	6			11			16	
Ski Touring						11				
Weak Layers		3		7				14	17	18
Feedback				8					17	18
Rescue	1				9					
Triggers			5	7 8 9	10 11			14		19 20
Snowmobile										
Terrain			5		10	11 12			16	18
Avi Control			6	7 8 9				14		20
Weather		3					13			
Route Finding						11 12		15		

Glossary

AEP – Avalanche Expertise Project. A collection of scenarios from experts to enhance development of cognitive avalanche skills.

AST – Avalanche Skills Training courses provided by Avalanche Canada.

CAA – Canadian Avalanche Association is a non-profit organization that supports avalanche practitioners in Canada by organizing professional training courses, providing a system for information exchange and ensures that members meet the highest practise standards to secure confidence in their avalanche safety programs.

CTA – Cognitive Task Analysis helps unpack the thought processes of experts, so they can be taught to others.

DPWL – Deep Persistent Weak Layer. a weak layer in the usually at or near the base of the snowpack, that resists forming a strong bond to neighbouring grains in the snowpack over an extended time period. It can be composed of surface hoar, facets, or depth hoar. A deep persistent slab problem often leads to a low-probability/high-consequence scenario, where the chances of triggering an avalanche are slim, but the destructive potential of any that are triggered is great.

InfoEx - The CAA's Industry Information Exchange (InfoEx®) is a daily exchange of technical snow, weather, avalanche and terrain information between subscribers.

PWL - A persistent weak layer is a weak layer in the snowpack that resists forming a strong bond to neighbouring grains in the snowpack over an extended time period. They can be composed of surface hoar, facets, or depth hoar.

Thoughts and Quotes – Snippets of Wisdom from Experts

Every supervisor and contemporary, really whoever spoke with an incident participant, has had an opportunity to influence their judgement, so a little bit of all of us goes with every incident that happens.

As a novice, you do not realize how small an avalanche can be to cause you trouble.

"Good judgment is usually the result of experience, and experience frequently the result of bad judgment". Robert Lovett

In heliski you change your terrain. In avalanche control you get rid of the danger.

In team decision making I say "Argue like you are right, listen like you are wrong, and be prepared the change your perspective at any time."

"It is better to be vaguely right than precisely wrong." J.M. Keynes

Many errors are that of perception not logic.

Confidence operates on a thin line. Possessed too little and you'll never take enough risk. Possessed too much and you will inevitably take imprudent risks. This is why, as with most things in life, having the right balance is critical

Stay humble and think holistically.

"Life gets so much easier when people like you." Neal Foard

Courage is knowing it might hurt and doing it anyway. Stupidity is the same. That's why life is hard.

Decisions are made by the soul. The brain is the marketing department not the decision making leader. Amygdala drives choices. Think about the least bad rather than shooting for the best.

Ski to the terrain not the hazard rating.

I don't think people start to really realize the consequences until they have something happen to them or really close to them.

Client management - it's the attitude that you put out that determines their attitude.

Risk acceptance is variable depending on the time of day.

As ski guides and pilots we always want to leave ourselves an out.

Do not negotiate with that little voice. I learned to not negotiate away the hazard.

Sometimes all you can attribute to the basis of a decision is a feeling.

Sometimes you have to miss a lot of good skiing so that you can have a life long enough to enjoy a lot of skiing.

Having radios in the group has just been a game changer. This is probably the one best thing that you can do, just remember to get on the radio.

Terrain is the solution, snowpack is the problem.

Nonevent feedback is the right answer with the wrong thinking.

We're always on the hunt for that that instability.

You aren't born with integrity and character. You build it.

"90% of all errors are that of perception not logic." David Perkins.

Consequences are the best teacher.

"Sipping" – acting through "Self-Induced Pressure".

Tracks are not necessarily a sign of intelligent life

When there's an absence of perfect information, emotion, passion, and tribal identity fill the void.

Uncertainty is painful to accept. It's far more comfortable to form a complete narrative about how things work. In a quest to leave no question unanswered, emotion gladly fills the holes left by a lack of information.

The mark of an expert is the ability to lose on purpose.

Don't leave good skiing to look for good skiing.

People who cut corners light a stick of dynamite. They don't stop at one short cut, deceitful action, or fib. It's a matter of when, not if, they blow up.

Careful that when you have a theory and the pieces don't fit, that you don't change the pieces instead of the theory.

Intuition will tell the thinking mind where to look next.– Jonas Salk

"Advice is what we ask for when we already know the answer but wish we didn't." E. Jong

"Change before you have to." – Jack Welch

Resulting – Equating the quality of the decision with the outcome.

Being taught is just the start. Learning is time invested through experience in what you have been taught. Teaching is the seed, experience is the growth.

Non-event Feedback - Doing the wrong thing and getting the right answer.

The chief trick to making good mistakes is not to hide them – especially not from yourself.

The worst nightmare for a forecaster is the post control release.

Darned iPads. Look out the window.

You should recognize when you know something and you still do the wrong thing.

A safety margin is also built on our ability to respond quickly.

People who cut corners light a stick of dynamite. They don't stop at one short cut, deceitful action, or fib. It's a matter of when, not if, they blow up.

As a novice, you do not realize how small an avalanche can be to cause you trouble.

The expert is always thinking "What if?" What if something happens?

I don't increase the risk based on feeling. I need a solid rational explanation.

If you don't know, you don't go.

You will never know if you are correct until you are wrong.

The lesser experienced/educated/skilled don't see the nuances.

Some of the decisions that are made by the guide are made for the guide as opposed to for that for the clients.

"Good luck is something you make and bad luck is something you endure." Rose Kennedy

Develop an option mindset by thinking "I Can do this but with these constraints"- not the limiting mindset of "I Can't do this because of those limitations."

"Life is hard man, but it's harder if you are stupid."   Jackie Brown

Many thanks to the avalanche professionals who took the time to be part of the Avalanche Expertise Project.

Tony Walker

helicourse@gmail.com

Printed in Great Britain
by Amazon